SIGNS OF PARASITISM

As must now be apparent, parasites can affect the health of reptiles in a variety of ways. The following are some of the symptoms which can be associated with parasitism.

General signs of parasitism in reptiles are·
1) Anorexia (refusal to feed)
2) Weight loss
3) Inactivity/lethargy
4) Failure to grow/thrive
5) Reproductive failure

Specific signs of parasitism in reptiles are:
1) Vomiting/regurgitation
2) Diarrhea
   a) mucus-laden stools
   b) bloody stools
   c) off color/sour odor stools
3) Dehydration/emaciation
4) Anorexia
5) Depression/agitation
6) Neurological abnormalities
7) Death

Means by which parasites harm their hosts:
1) Suck blood (hookworms) or promote exudates (lungworms)
2) Cause blood loss
   a) actual removal (hookworms)
   b) nutritional deficiency
   c) hemolytic crisis
3) Feed on solid tissues (liver flukes)
4) Compete with the host for food it has ingested
   a) ingest intestinal contents (roundworms)
   b) absorb intestinal contents directly through the parasite's body wall (tapeworms)
5) Destroy host's cells (coccidia)
6) Mechanical obstruction of the intestine (roundworms), bile ducts (roundworms, tapeworms, flukes), blood vessels (filarids, flukes),

bronchi (lungworms), and other body channels
7) Production of various toxic substances (hemolysins, histolysins, and anticoagulants, etc.)
8) Trigger allergic reactions
9) Loss of intestinal contents due to host malabsorption
10) Cause reactions in the host
  a) inflammation
  b) infection (usually bacterial)
  c) hyperplasia
  d) nodule formation (usually granulomatous) in any affected tissue
  e) hypertrophy (swelling)
11) Carry other diseases (mites, ticks)
12) Trigger the development of cancer
13) Reduce host's immunosuppression (resistance to other diseases)

> *"The number one reason for failure to successfully maintain and breed natricine snakes to date is untreated parasitism."*
> John Rossi, D.V.M., M.A. (1992)

PARASITES: IMPACT ON CAPTIVE REPRODUCTION

Reproduction is a function afforded those individuals whose health allows for more than basic survival. As has been touched on, a heavily parasitized reptile is not a prime candidate for efficient reproduction. Parasites that steal or inhibit the absorption of foodstuffs create a malnourished animal. Even parasites that annoy the host may physiologically impair reproduction. This concept was proven by Dinardo (1992), whose study of lizards illustrated how stress depleted stores of corticosterones (hormones that handle stress in the body) and reduced reproductive hormones to near zero levels. A reptile with a heavy parasite load is stressed. A stressed reptile will not and cannot reproduce.

UNDERSTANDING REPTILE PARASITES

A Basic Manual for
Herpetoculturists & Veterinarians

Roger J. Klingenberg D.V.M.

Table of Contents

Introduction

While the mortality rate in reptile collections has decreased due to improved herpetocultural practices, it is still a very significant problem. Have you ever stopped to consider the main causes of death in captive reptiles? Based on autopsy results performed by the author over the course of fifteen years, the top three causes of death in order of occurrence are: 1) nutritional, 2) bacterial, and 3) parasitic. This has also been confirmed by other researchers. In a review of records, Griner in 1983 found that parasitic lesions were second only to bacterial lesions among necropsy findings in captive reptiles. A paper by R. Ippen (1972) revealed that in necropsies performed on over 1100 reptiles from their zoological park 40% of the specimens were actively infested and in 79% of these cases parasites were incriminated as the cause of death!

These shocking statistics point out the fact that parasites are often not recognized as a cause of disease. Indeed, parasites are often quite insidious. As will be illustrated in this book, parasites are very significant in captive conditions where they can reach catastrophic levels. Large groups of reptiles housed together are particularly at risk. Whether they own one reptile or hundreds, the control of parasites should be a primary concern to all herpetoculturists.

This book is intended to help the average herpetoculturist, amateur or professional, maintain parasite-free collections. It is not intended to be an extensive compilation of parasite taxonomy (Appendix I lists sources for those so inclined). The goals are twofold. One is to provide an understanding of, and ability to apply, basic principles in the identification, diagnosis, and treatment of common reptilian parasites. The other goal is to convey an understanding of how captivity + stress + parasites = disease, and ways this scenario can be avoided or treated.

Parasites: Why Bother?

It is a known fact that parasites cause and contribute to disease processes in reptiles. Despite this, many herpetoculturists' view is that if they are not seeing problems, then why look? "If it ain't broke, why fix it?", so to speak. At the other extreme, many reptile owners routinely "shotgun" every animal they acquire with every drug they deem appropriate. While this book will present information on dosage and administration of safe parasiticidal drugs, it is always optimal to base treatment on a known problem.

Animal rights supporters and anti-pet organizations will passionately argue that reptiles should not be subjected to confinement; rather, they should be enjoyed from afar. This point of view fails to consider the deep-rooted needs many humans have for interrelationships with the natural world. Many people, the author included, own and maintain captive reptiles. Many species have proven highly adaptable to captivity. As responsible herpetoculturists, we owe it to the animals in our care to provide the best possible standards of captive maintenance, if not for altruistic reasons, then for the personal and economic benefits of maintaining healthy reptiles.

Many reptile owners claim to have never lost a single animal to a parasite-related death. This may be due to the simple fact that they didn't know what to look for. The following examples are a small sampling of parasite-related or -induced problems that have actually happened in herpetocultural collections:

1) A snake with loose and smelly diarrhea, spotted with occasional blood, still eats and eventually breeds. It is found dead the morning after breeding.
2) A tick-infested python develops a generalized bacterial infection, despite the removal of the ticks.
3) An iguana with mites develops a small area of "scale rot" that escalates into a massive skin infection.
4) A snake with chronic regurgitation fails to gain adequate weight, and subsequent breeding efforts fail.

5) A box turtle infested with maggots associated with biting fly wounds subsequently develops abscesses, leading to anorexia, a failure to thrive, and eventual death.

6) A kingsnake delivers one good clutch of eggs, and having resumed eating, dies shortly thereafter, gravid with a second clutch.

7) A rosy boa with a firm, mid-body swelling and occasional regurgitation consequently dies suddenly.

8) A gecko with mites develops a severe conjunctivitis and subsequent rubbing of the eye causes severe corneal damage. The eye has to be removed surgically.

What is the common thread among all these actual cases? A **parasite** was instrumental in each. From external parasites such as ticks and mites, to internal parasites such as _Cryptosporidium_ and protozoans, reptiles can be affected in ways ranging from mild nuisance to fatal implications.

This ball python was infested with six kinds of parasites: mites, ticks, three types of nematodes, and tapeworms. Such parasite loads are typical with many imported reptiles and can overwhelm the host in a captive situation. Photo by the author.

As the captive breeding of reptiles becomes more commonplace, herpetoculturists are striving to develop methods for achieving increased breeding efficiency in their animals. A variety of areas are currently being investigated, including nutrition, better thermal regulation, copulatory cycling and timing, egg incubation temperatures, and many more. The host-parasite relationship is one such topic the herpetoculturist cannot afford to overlook.

African fat-tail gecko (*Hemitheconyx caudicinctus*). Imported specimens have a significantly greater survival rate if treated for parasites, particularly flagellate protozoans. Photo by Philippe de Vosjoli.

Basic Parasite Terminology

For herpetoculturists to understand the possible effects of parasites in captive reptiles, it will be essential to have a basic understanding of parasite life cycles and associated terminology. All parasites require a **host,** an animal upon or within which they live or complete their life cycle. The **definitive host** is a host in which the life cycle of a particular parasite can be completed by reproduction. A **dead end host** is an animal upon or within which a parasite may temporarily live, but cannot complete its life cycle. Many parasites require more than one host to complete their life cycles, having one or more **intermediate hosts.** Parasites not requiring an intermediate host to produce viable offspring are said to have a **direct life cycle.** Those requiring one or more intermediate hosts are said to have an **indirect life cycle.**

An example is in order. The hookworm is a nematode parasite with many definitive hosts. These worms can reproduce equally well in a turtle or a snake, each of which is a definitive host. Hookworms produce eggs released in the feces of infected definitive hosts, and these eggs hatch to produce larvae which can re-infect the same individuals by being ingested in contaminated food/water or by percutaneous (through the skin) invasion. This illustrates a direct life cycle, as it doesn't require an intermediate host to re-enter the host animal or another host of the same species.

Indirect life cycles are characteristic of the ascarids. For example, roundworms may affect many definitive hosts, but the eggs passed in the stools of an infected animal will not re-infect that animal unless the larvae are ingested by an intermediate host, such as a fish or amphibian, which in turn can re-infest the original host only if ingested. Roundworms can, in rare instances, cause disease in humans, but they cannot reproduce in humans. On the other hand, roundworms in a snake or turtle can produce viable offspring to pass on. Thus, humans are dead end hosts for roundworms.

7

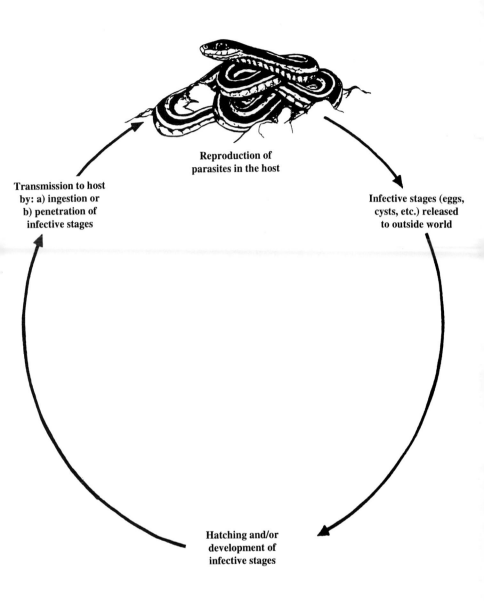

Reproduction of
parasites in the host

Transmission to host
by: a) ingestion or
b) penetration of
infective stages

Infective stages (eggs,
cysts, etc.) released
to outside world

Hatching and/or
development of
infective stages

EXAMPLE OF DIRECT LIFE CYCLE

The significance of direct and indirect (life cycle) parasites is extremely important and will be elaborated upon in later sections. Hopefully, the aforementioned example makes it clear that the snake with hookworms (direct life cycle) can re-infest itself simply by exposure to its own feces. The snake with roundworms can only re-infest itself if the intermediate host (the fish or amphibian in this example) is present as well.

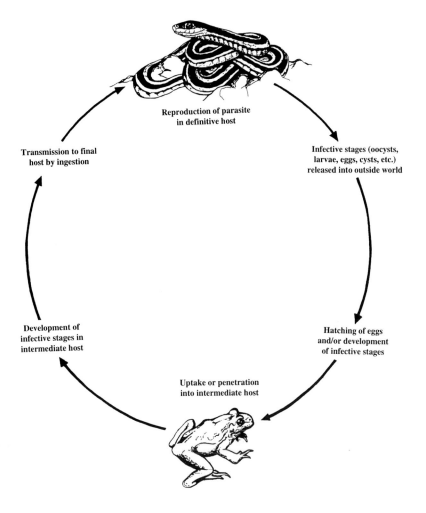

EXAMPLE OF INDIRECT LIFE CYCLE

Diagnostic Procedures

Hopefully, by now I have convinced the reader of the importance and potential damage caused by parasites. Then how do we diagnose their presence?

DETERMINING THE PRESENCE OF EXTERNAL PARASITES

External parasites such as ticks, mites, etc., are generally seen with the naked eye. Recently fed ticks are engorged and protrude from under or around the scales. However, immature forms of ticks may hide under scales and avoid detection. On inspection of a reptile, pay special attention to flat or slightly raised, circular objects protruding from under a scale.

Reptile mites are small, but can be observed moving on the host. When in doubt, the reptile can be placed over a white piece of paper and rubbed, whereupon the mites that fall off will be seen moving on the paper. The appearance of white flecking or thick white "dust" particles on a snake or lizard is a reliable indicator of the presence of mites. The white flecks are actually mite feces. The application of moist paper towel along the areas where these feces are present will usually pick up live mites and confirm their presence. Water containers can be examined for drowned mites, as mite-infested reptiles often spend an inordinate amount of time in their water containers in an attempt to rid themselves of these parasites. Snakes with deep labial pits or grooves, such as emerald tree boas, will often dip their entire heads under water to try to eliminate mites hidden in these natural crevices. Patches of dry skin or crusty material around the eye or protruding eye rims should alert the keeper to look for mites.

INTERNAL PARASITES;
DETERMINING THEIR PRESENCE

Whenever possible, fecal samples should be obtained directly from the animal in question. If fresh stools cannot be obtained this way, an effort should be made to obtain as fresh a sample as possible. In some cases, the author instructs his clients to refrigerate the sample in an airtight plastic bag overnight. Sample containers should be as water- and air-tight as possible. The lack of oxygen will inhibit the development of pre-parasitic stages. Refrigeration will also prevent the rapid development of eggs into larvae at elevated temperatures. Dehydration of the sample is to be strictly avoided as the fragile parasitic stages (eggs, larvae, oocysts, etc.) may be disrupted. Some people advise that the parasitic stages be fixed in a 10% formaldehyde solution, but the author prefers non-formaldehyde treated samples.

Why all the fuss over the sample? Most reptile parasites are fairly stable, but some parasites such as protozoans, coccidial oocysts, and certain worm larval forms will perish if exposed to drying or temperature extremes.

Once the sample is obtained, it is examined according to one of the following procedures:
A) **Direct smears** - A small amount of fecal material is applied to a microscope slide, mixed with a few drops of physiological saline or distilled water, and a cover slip applied. Stains like new methylene blue, and Lugol's iodine may help to contrast difficult to visualize parasites, such as protozoans. Frye (1991) suggests adding a few drops of merthiolate (available at a drugstore). This procedure may kill protozoans, but by staining the protozoans and some parasite ova it will be easier to observe them. The physiological saline will stimulate the protozoans to move due to the increased concentration of the saline solution. Using the merthiolate or Lugol's iodine will help stain them, but will also kill the protozoans so motion must be evaluated relative to the solution or stains used. Due to small sample size, smears are often unrewarding for diagnosing most parasites, but will be the method of choice for diagnosing protozoans.

B) **Fecal flotation** - The principle of differential flotation is based on the fact that the eggs of parasitic worms will float in certain solutions in which a mass of fecal debris will not (see illustration on how to perform flotation). By allowing the eggs to float to the surface of the solution it concentrates them and allows identification. The addition of a few drops of merthiolate (Frye) or Lugol's iodine (author's

11

preference) to the flotation medium will allow for better observation of protozoans and some ova. The Lugol's iodine works best if mixed with the fecal matter before adding the flotation solution.

If fecal samples are found to be void of parasites, and yet a high index of suspicion exists, then other methods can be used: A) cloacal smears or flushes may produce richer materials for examination; B) stomach flushes may also be examined; or C) sputum occasionally will reveal parasitic evidence, especially if respiratory symptoms are seen. Cloacal smears/flushes and stomach flushes are usually performed and evaluated by a veterinarian or other trained person .

FECAL FLOTATION SOLUTIONS

1) Sodium Nitrate - This is the most common type used and can be purchased pre-made in gallons at veterinary supply stores. Fecasol® is a common name brand.

2) Zinc Sulfate - This is probably the choice of flotation solutions, but is harder to prepare. Zinc sulfate powder is added to water until a hydrometer reading of 1.20 on the specific gravity scale is reached. To help identify protozoans a few drops of Lugol's iodine can be added to the fecal material and stirred in with it before the addition of the zinc sulfate. The Lugol's iodine tends to stain the protozoans for easier identification.

3) Saturated sugar solution - These solutions are easy to prepare by simply adding sugar to heated water until no more will dissolve. The liquid should be heated to near boiling, but need not actually boil. One recipe calls for 1 lb. of granulated sugar added to 12 fluid ounces of tap water and heated until the mixture is clear. This solution is not considered to be as good as the first two listed. Fungal/mold growth is a problem, but adding a few drops of phenol or household bleach helps control the fungal growth. Refrigeration of the solution between uses also slows fungal growth. The main advantage to this flotation solution is that it can be easily and inexpensively prepared at home. The main disadvantage, however, is that it attracts ants and other insect vermin. It is also sticky.

Flotation technique for concentrating eggs and other parasitic stages

Fecal flotation is based on the principle of differences in specific gravity. When feces are mixed in liquids of high specific gravity and allowed to stand, the worm eggs, oocysts, and protozoal cysts float to the top while the heavy fecal debris sinks to the bottom. The top film of concentrated material can then be removed and examined.

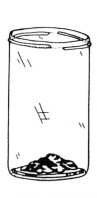	
1) A lump of feces the size of a raisin is placed in a pill vial	2) The vial is filled 2/3 full with the flotation solution and stirred vigorously to break up the fecal material

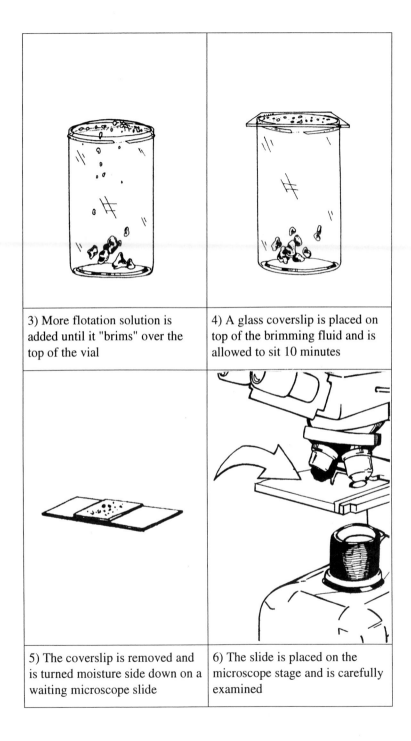

3) More flotation solution is added until it "brims" over the top of the vial	4) A glass coverslip is placed on top of the brimming fluid and is allowed to sit 10 minutes
5) The coverslip is removed and is turned moisture side down on a waiting microscope slide	6) The slide is placed on the microscope stage and is carefully examined

Equipment Required

By now, the reader will have decided on one of two courses of action:

A) He or she will elect to take their samples to an appropriate lab, such as their veterinarian. If nothing else, this booklet may assist your veterinarian, especially one who is not very experienced in reptilian diseases, to help diagnose parasitic problems.

B) He or she will learn to examine fecal samples, not only to save money, but to expedite things and satisfy his or her scientific interests. The following description of equipment requirements is for these individuals.

THE MICROSCOPE

The most important instrument for recognizing parasites is the microscope. For professionals spending hours a week viewing, it is advisable to invest in a high quality binocular scope (viewed with both eyes), equipped with a mechanical (moving) stage. However, the advanced amateur can get by nicely with a simple microscope that won't bankrupt their hobby. The following features are desirable:

A) **Monocular vs. binocular** - Monocular microscopes allow viewing through one eyepiece, so the user views with one eye only. Monocular is fine for limited viewing, though headaches and double vision can result from extended periods of use. If viewing more than an hour on a routine basis, and 3D imaging is desired, then binocular is a must.

B) **Movable vs. non-movable stages** - Movable stages (the platform the slide with the sample sits on) allow for more precise movement of the slide while viewing. Non-movable or hand-operated stages require practice, but again are very workable.

C) **Objectives** - The objectives refer to the power through which you will magnify the observed objects. Most <u>eyepieces</u> have a standard l0x magnification, but l0x and 40x objectives are also needed. To obtain the final magnification, the eyepiece magnification is multiplied by the objective used. Thus, the l0x eyepiece looking through a l0x objective results in a l00x magnification. Magnifications of l00x are a must, but 400x are desirable. Higher objectives (l00x) are required to find the smallest of protozoan parasites.

D) **Light sources** - A built-in light source is the best for uniformity of lighting; however, mirror reflector models will often suffice.

E) **Phase contrast** - This is an optional feature that allows more or less light which often greatly improves the quality of illumination. Phase contrast will also necessitate better and more expensive objectives.

Confused? The point is that a basic monocular model with a non-movable stage, l0x and 40x objectives, and a mirror reflector will suffice for basic diagnostics. All options that increase ease and accuracy of the microscope also increase the price. Please refer to Appendix II for sources of microscopes.

The other required equipment consists of microscope slides and cover slips, fecal flotation solutions, and fecal flotation vials. These are relatively inexpensive and usually can be obtained from your local veterinary supply outlets or a cooperative reptile veterinarian. Stains such as Mayer's hematoxylin and Lugol's iodine are desirable, but the merthiolate suggested by Frye is an easily obtained, effective alternative.

THE MICROSCOPE

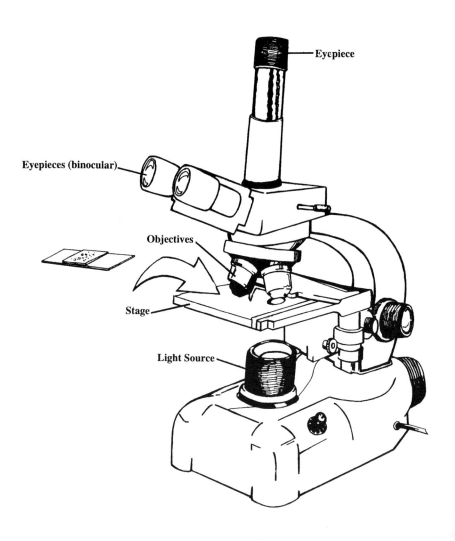

After material from fecal flotation has collected on a coverslip, it is placed upside down on a glass slide which is then examined under the microscope. **Illustration by Glenn Warren.**

Parasites:
To Treat or Not to Treat?

Reptiles typically harbor a wide variety of both internal and external parasites. This parasite burden is often heavy and every body surface and organ system may be affected by either larval or adult stages of the parasites. The parasite burden may also be light and self-limiting in nature. Some parasites are harmful to their hosts; others are not. Furthermore, a parasite that might be harmful in large numbers might not be harmful in smaller numbers. How can we determine the probable impact of parasites if parasitism is so common? How do we determine the clinical significance of evidence of parasitism?

To answer these questions we need to quickly review the information on life cycles and also look at the differences between an animal in captivity and one in the wild.

In general, the parasites most successful in propagating themselves are those doing the least harm to their hosts. The perfect parasite would prefer a state of mutual benefit or a symbiotic relationship with their host. Obviously, a parasite won't do well through time if the demise of the host is an immediate goal, unless there is a neverending supply of hosts.

The parasites with the most potential to cause harm are those with a direct life cycle. Let's reiterate the salient points of direct life cycles. The adult parasite with a direct life cycle produces a life form, be it larvae, eggs, oocysts, etc., that can regain access to the host by being ingested or in some cases by burrowing in through the skin. These parasites have the ways and means to gain easy access to the host if the opportunity arises.

As noted previously, most wild-caught reptiles have parasites, and yet the majority of these animals are healthy and probably do not require treatment. They harbor parasites and manage to survive in the wild in a more or less healthy state. How can that be?

This brings us to what the author feels is the key point of parasitism and treatment. Reptiles in the wild live a fairly nomadic lifestyle, searching for food and shelter on a daily basis. Rarely will these creatures return to the exact same location or area, and even if they do, it will occasionally be altered by rain, wind, etc. In captivity, however, reptiles typically are forced to spend inordinate amounts of time in a limited area, perhaps with only a single shelter, a water dish, a climbing limb, etc. The captive environment, because of limited space, can thus significantly increase the probability of re-exposure of the host to external (i.e., mites) or internal (i.e., hookworms) parasites. Thus, captivity can provide the direct life cycle parasite with the opportunity to overwhelm its host.

As an example, a bullsnake in my native state of Colorado may spend most of its time hiding in burrows of other animals, such as prairie dogs, gophers, etc. Early morning and early afternoon when the heat is adequate, but not overwhelming, it hunts for food. Let us assume that our bullsnake friend has three parasites: 1) hookworms (nasty intestinal worms with a direct life cycle), 2) roundworms (intestinal worms with an indirect life cycle), and 3) snake mites (an external bug with a direct life cycle). As the snake actively searches for its meals each day, it occasionally will defecate. Each fecal mass passes the eggs of the hookworms and roundworms on to the environment. However, because our friend is on the move and generally finds a new home or rarely defecates in his routine haunts, the probability of re-exposure to his parasites is limited. The hookworm eggs, which hatch into larvae that can penetrate skin or gain access by oral routes, have little chance of direct reinfection due to proximity. They must try to gain access to some other host. The roundworm eggs would have to cycle through another intermediate host before re-infesting the bullsnake so they are even less a threat. As our bullsnake beds down for the night, some of the blood-sucking mites abandon the snake to lay their eggs, often numbering in the hundreds. It will be days or weeks before the mite eggs hatch (depending on the tempera-ture) and the bullsnake will be gone long before that. The important points are: 1) mobile reptiles do not readily provide parasites with direct life cycles the opportunity to reinfect them and build up their numbers; 2) parasites with indirect life cycles can only build up if the

19

host is extremely infested or the host has ready access to the required intermediate hosts; and 3) parasites harmful in large numbers may not be in small numbers. **Many parasitic problems in nature are self-limiting.** Our bullsnake friend could live his entire life with few effects from his parasitic problems. However, those very same parasites which may be self-limiting in nature tend to build up under the conditions of captivity.

Let's put our bullsnake in a 2 x 3 x 1 ft. cage and hypothesize the same group of parasites. Our snake now has to defecate in a limited area, and consequently can 1) lie in feces, 2) defecate in a water dish, or 3) drag feces over surfaces and into contact with food/water, etc. The hookworms, with a direct life cycle hatching from the eggs in the feces, can gain access to the host either by penetrating the skin or via the oral route, either through contaminated water or food. The roundworms, having an indirect life cycle, cannot threaten the host with further build-up in this particular case, due to the lack of an intermediate host. The mites, on the other hand, can lay their hundreds of eggs in the enclosure; the resulting hatchlings will have a guaranteed meal ticket nearby. Thus, the hookworms and mites could build to massive levels, taxing the health of the host. The roundworms, although not increasing in numbers, will be able to further tax the declining health of the weakening host.

How else does captivity aid parasites besides simple opportunity? Captivity-induced **stress** also tends to change the balance of the host/ parasite relationship which can result in disease. Such stress factors include crowding, inadequate heat or light, poor hiding areas (lack of security), substrate problems, altered diets, etc. All these factors suppress the immune system of the host and make the individual more susceptible to the effects of infestation.

To summarize, I sincerely believe **captivity** and **captivity-related stress** to be responsible for parasite infestations, self-limiting in nature, becoming pathogenic in captivity. In general, parasites with **direct** life cycles will increase disproportionately in captive speci-mens. Parasites with indirect life cycles will be less likely to increase in numbers or be transmitted within a colony due to nonavailability of suitable intermediate hosts. However, as we have discussed, even parasites with indirect life cycles can cause harm if present in large numbers or if the host is weakened by captivity-induced stress. Additionally, certain food items offered, such as fish or frogs, can serve as intermediate hosts for some parasites and thus become another potential source of parasites.

PARASITES + CAPTIVITY + STRESS = DISEASE POTENTIAL

Because of the risk factors associated with captivity and the availability of relatively safe and effective compounds to treat both internal and external parasites, it has become my practice to **eliminate all parasites in captive specimens**. I feel we owe it to these captive creatures, who depend on us for their care, to eliminate the possibility of parasitic disease as a stress factor in their lives. I also feel it is imperative that herpetoculturists provide captive conditions helpful to the overall welfare of these animals.

Red-eared slider (*Trachemys scripta elegans*). Many wild caught water turtles are infested with several parasites. As with tortoises, an easy way to treat them is to mix the appropriate drug in their food. Photo by Philippe de Vosjoli.

Treating Reptilian Parasites

There have been very few controlled studies of anthelmintics and insecticides used in reptiles. Because of this, many of the widely published doses are empirical and have been passed on through the literature for decades. The following drugs and doses provided are based on both unpublished research by the author (Appendix III for synopsis) and over fifteen years of use by the author in exotic animal practice. A chart has been provided, listing most of the drugs in past and current literature with comments on their use.

Prior to presenting the specific treatments, we need to discuss the drugs, medications, and insecticides that will be suggested for use in your reptiles.

CHEMOTHERAPEUTICS FOR PARASITES AND
PARASITIC DISEASES:
The ideal anthelmintics and insecticides for parasite treatment would be: 1) highly effective, 2) very safe, 3) easy to use and, hopefully, 4) inexpensive. These are the criteria the author has used to pick and choose among the myriad of available chemotherapeutic agents.

In the author's opinion, the following drugs are the only ones needed to control 99% of reptilian parasites and fit the aforementioned criteria better than the rest. These drugs are:

1) Fenbendazole (Panacur®)
2) Praziquantel (Droncit®)
3) Metronidazole (Flagyl®)
4) Sulfadimethoxine (Albon®)
5) 2,2-dichlorvinyl dimethylphosphate (No-Pest® strip)
   a) similar products
6) Trichlorfon concentrate (Neguvon®)
7) Ivermectin (Ivomec®)

Fenbendazole (Panacur®)

Panacur® is a member of the important benzimidazole group of anthelmintics which also includes Thiabendazole (TBZ) and Mebendazole (Telmin). Panacur® is a broad-spectrum anthelmintic that has a direct effect on adult parasites, some activity against migrating larvae, and ovicidal effects brought on by the prompt sterilization of the adult worms. Having effects on migrating larvae, and sterilizing adults so no more eggs are passed, are very important properties. Most anthelmintics are active against adults only.

This group of drugs is extremely safe, with Panacur® having a margin of safety up to 5,000 times normal dose in mammals. To the author's knowledge, a reptilian death directly associated with the use of Panacur® in snakes, lizards, or turtles has never been reported.

The author uses Panacur® suspension (100 mg/ml) at the dosage of 25 mg/kg or 10 mg/lb, given orally once every 2 weeks. It generally requires a minimum of three treatments to eliminate nematode parasites. Because such a small volume is required (0.1 ml/lb), the author usually administers this drug with a round-tipped feeding needle, passed to the back of the throat (see illustration). It can also be administered to turtles and tortoises by mixing it with their feed.

Panacur ® is the drug of choice for nematode parasites. While it also exerts an effect on tapeworms (cestodes), it is not the drug of choice for them.

Praziquantel (Droncit®)

Various drugs for use with tapeworms are listed in the literature. The drug of choice is Droncit®, which is dosed at 5 mg/kg, either as an injectable or as a tablet crushed and mixed with a liquid and tubed. Droncit® has also shown some efficacy against extra-intestinal forms of tapeworms and also against flukes.

Metronidazole (Flagyl®)

Flagyl® is an anti-bacterial agent of considerable use in treating disturbances of intestinal flora. Flagyl® will suppress or eliminate unwanted populations of bacteria or protozoa, with minimal harmful effects on useful gastrointestinal microbial flora. It is considered the drug of choice for most, if not all, protozoan and amoebic infections in reptiles.

Flagyl® is considered to be a fairly safe drug, but serious blood defects and liver problems have been noted in mammals. While no specific data proves teratogenic (birth defects) effects, administration of this drug to gravid reptiles is not recommended. Jacobsen (1988) reports deaths in indigo snakes at dosages above 100 mg/kg while dosages at 40 mg/kg have been given safely. Jarchow has reported deaths in *Lampropeltis zonata* and *L. pyromelena* at doses above 100 mg/kg.

The author prefers to use the Flagyl® suspension (Flagenase 400, available in Mexico) over the tablets. It is easier to measure and administer the liquid, and easier to ensure precise dosage to small reptiles. Tablets can be ground up and mixed with water, but the drug is not water soluble and can be more difficult to dose properly.

The author doses Flagyl® at 25 - 50 mg/kg or 10 - 25 mg/lb, given once and repeated three to four days later, if needed. It should be noted that several sources in the literature suggest using doses as high as 125 - 275 mg/kg! In light of toxic reactions in some reptiles, it seems inappropriate to use a dose that could be toxic even to some mammals. The author has found the lower recommended dose to work as well as the higher dose, so why take chances?

Flagyl® has also been touted by some herpetoculturists as an "appetite stimulant." There is no evidence to suggest that this drug has any properties to directly stimulate appetite. It may possibly stimulate appetite indirectly by correcting an inappropriate bacterial flora, eliminating protozoal flare-ups in the GI tract, or eliminating sub-clinical amoebic populations (Frye, 1991).

Sulfadimethoxine (Alhon®) or Sulfamethoxine (Bactrovet®)
These are the current drugs of choice for coccidial infections. These sulfa drugs are both anti-bacterial and anti-coccidial. They are considered very safe, but should be used with caution in severely dehydrated animals in which renal function would be a concern. The author uses a daily dose of 50 mg/kg or 20 mg/lb orally for three consecutive days, stops for three days, and then repeats the same dosage for another three days. This drug can be administered in prey animals if the animal being treated is feeding, but this is not the method the author prefers. It requires daily feeding and the food may interfere with the drug absorption and cause the drug to accumulate.

2,2-dichlorovinyl dimethylphosphate strips
No-Pest® strips, and similar products, have been used for many years for the treatment of mites and in the author's experience have proven very safe. The author has had clients who, by exposing the reptiles continuously to the vapors have seen toxic signs, which were reversible when removed. Reports of reptile deaths have been attributed to the use of these strips.

The use of these strips will be greatly expanded upon in the section on treating mites. However, proper usage is dependent on 1) using a bubble gum size piece per 10 cubic feet, 2) avoiding direct contact with the reptile by placing the piece in a small container with holes, 3) using the No-Pest® piece two or three times weekly for three to four weeks for only two to three hours at a time, and 4) allowing for ventilation in cage.

Trichlorfon
Trichlorfon is an organophosphate product sold on the market as a cattle dip. A study by Boyer (1992) at the Dallas Zoo indicated that a 0.15% solution has proven to be safe and effective. In their study, 1 of 600 snakes in the study died. They also used the spray on green iguanas, chuckwallas, and collared lizards. Geckos were found not to tolerate the insecticide. The specific usage of this drug will be expanded on in the mite treatment section.

Ivermectin - (Ivomec®)
Ivermectin is one of a group of parasiticides initially developed for use in the treatment and control of internal and external parasites in cattle and horses. Now it is also one of the most widely recommended heartworm preventative products used in our pet dogs. The theory behind the use of ivermectin in reptiles is that very low circulating levels of the drug will treat filarial nematodes (rare), intestinal parasites, and mites and ticks feeding on the blood of the treated animal. The current recommended dosages are 0.2 mg/kg or 0.02 ml/kg, once every two weeks. Using a product like Ivomec®, which is a 1% solution (10 mg/cc), means we need to give approximately 0.01 ml per pound. This translates roughly into a small drop of the undiluted solution per pound.

While ivermectin has shown itself to be very safe in snakes and lizards, it is hard to determine the proper dosage. The author feels that this drug should not be used in animals smaller than 1 lb. unless it is based on very accurate dilutions and even then caution is advised. **Ivermectin is absolutely contraindicated in all chelonians**. The drug apparently can cross the blood brain barrier of turtles/tortoises with ease and cause potentially irreversible and potentially fatal neurological disease.

Ivermectin has been the greatest disappointment of all current drugs to the author. It seemed to hold limitless potential and could be given orally or by injection (the author prefers oral route). However, the author has found in clinical use:
1) Panacur® works better at eliminating nematodes and offers a better range of safety (see Appendix III for study results);

2) Ivermectin has limited effects, if any, on tapeworms;
3) In the author's hands, ivermectin has not been effective in the elimination of mites and ticks.

Despite producing circulating blood and tissue levels which the mites and ticks will feed on, these external pests were not consistently eliminated. Two problems may exist with the use of ivermectin for this purpose. First, the dosage may not be adequate, but the author isn't willing to go to a higher level due to the potential for toxicity. Second, the author would hypothesize that circulating blood levels are not maintained long enough to allow all feeding mites or ticks to become exposed. Rosskopf (1992) recently reported that he has had good results in eliminating mites from snakes by giving subcutaneous injections dosed at 0.2 mg/kg, once a week for three weeks.

A more promising use of ivermectin for mite control was reported by Abrahams (1992). He mixed 1/2 cc of the 1% Ivomec® (MSD AGVET, 10 mg/cc) with 1 quart of tap water and sprayed environment and reptile. The author has tried this regimen only a dozen times or so, but it worked well. Abrahams reported that he had no mites present after one treatment, but in large groups of reptiles where mites are persistent, repeating applications once every 7-10 days would be logical.

Recommended uses for Ivermectin are:
1) Filarial nematodes (rare - found on blood smears)
2) *Rhabdias* and *Entomelas* nematodes (lungworms). Panacur ® at the high end of its dosage range also appears to be effective.
3) Nematode parasites resistant to Panacur®
4) For eliminating mites by using it in the spray form. This will require more research to validate the results, but it seems to have promise. The author again has had poor results using ivermectin as an injectable or oral product to eliminate mites.

Drugs Recommended for Parasiticidal Use in Reptiles

Parasite	Drug	Dosage -mg/kg	Comments
Protozoans			
Amoebas & Flagellates	Metronidazole (Flagyl-Searle)	25-40 mg/kg PO; repeat in 3-4 days if needed	Author prefers suspension available in Mexico for more accurate dosage. Do not exceed 40 mg/kg in tricolor snakes, indigos, or Uracoan rattlers (Funk).
Coccidia	Sulfadimethoxine (Albon-Roche) Sulfadiazine Sulfamerazine Sulfamethazine	50 mg/kg x 3 days, stop 3 days, then repeat x 3 days	Avoid usage in dehydrated or renal-impaired animals.
Metazoans			
Cestodes (Tapeworms)	Praziquantel (Droncit-Mobay)	5-8 mg/kg PO or IM; repeat in 2 weeks	Drug of choice for tapeworms over many other drugs available due to safety.
Trematodes (Flukes)	Praziquantel	5-8 mg/kg PO or IM; repeat in 2 weeks	
Nematodes	Fenbendazole (Panacur-Horchst Rousset)	25 mg/kg PO; repeat in 2 weeks	Drug of choice for all nematodes due to extremely large margin of safety.
	Ivermectin (Ivomec-Merck)	0.2 mg/kg or 0.02 ml/kg PO or IM; repeat in 2 weeks	Narrower range of safety. Use only if Panacur fails. Avoid usage in reptiles less than one pound in weight, due to dosage accuracy problems. Do not us in turtles or tortoises
Ectoparasites			
Mites	No-Pest Strips	6.0 mm per 10 cubic feet (Frye)	Place in container to avoid direct contact with reptile. Do not use continuously. Expose 2-3 hours, 2-3 times weekly for 3-4 weeks. Use with frequent cleaning/substrate changes.
	Trichlorfon (Chemtronics)	Dilute 8% stock to make 0.15% (add 8 ml of stock to 400 ml of water) (D.Boyer)	Spray reptile lightly including eyes & labial pits, avoiding mouth as much as possible. Ventilation is necessary, no airtight cages. Withhold water for 24 hrs. post spraying. Do not use with geckos.
Abbreviations:	IM intramuscular kg kilogram mg milligrams ml milliliter PO per os: orally		

27

Other drugs available for parasiticidal use in reptiles, but not recommended by the author

Drug Name	Potential Use	Sugg. Dosage	Comments
Fenbentel + praziquantel (Vercom-Mobay)	Nematodes & cestodes	2.3 ml/kg orally based on prazi-quantel at 8 mg/kg (Harvey/Clark)	2 of 25 iguanas in the study by Harvey & Clark died and did not eliminate the parasites.
		or 580 mg/kg PO x 3 days (Miller)	Can cause neurological damage in Calif. mtn. kingsnakes (per comm. B.Gillingham).
Niclosamide (Yomesan-Mobay)	Cestodes	150-300 mg/kg PO; repeat in 2 weeks	Droncit is better and safer and capable of eliminating extra-intestinal forms (Jacobson).
Bunamidine HCl (Scoloban-Mobay)	Cestodes	25-50 mg/kg PO; repeat in 2 weeks	Same as with Niclosamide.
Dichlorvos (Task-Shell)	Nematodes	12.5 mg/kg PO	This is an organophosphate that has an unacceptable margin of safety.
Levamisole HCl (Tramisol-Amer. Cyanamid)	Nematodes	5-10 mg/kg IC or subcutane-ously; repeat in 2 weeks	The only advantage of this drug is that it can be injected. Very narrow range of safety.
Levamisole Phos.(Ripercol-Amer.Cyanmid)	As above		
Thiabendazole (Thibenzole-Merck)	Nematodes	50-100 mg/kg PO, mixed to a liquid; repeat in 2 weeks	Author personally witnessed the deaths of an indigo snake and two bullsnakes.
Dimetridazole (Emtryl)	Protozoans	40 mg/kg PO; once daily for 5 days	Metronidazole (Flagyl) is very adequate, and Emtryl is being removed from the U.S. market.
Abbreviations	IC intracoelomic kg kilogram mg milligram ml milliliter PO per os: orally		

ADMINISTRATION OF DRUGS LESS THAN 1cc
USING A BALL-TIPPED SYRINGE

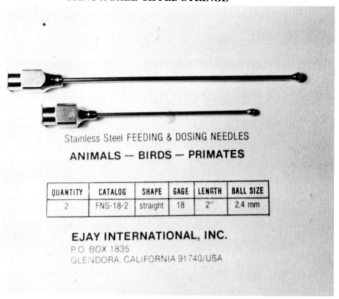

Stainless Steel FEEDING & DOSING NEEDLES

ANIMALS — BIRDS — PRIMATES

QUANTITY	CATALOG	SHAPE	GAGE	LENGTH	BALL SIZE
2	FNS-18-2	straight	18	2"	2.4 mm

EJAY INTERNATIONAL, INC.
P.O. BOX 1835
GLENDORA, CALIFORNIA 91740/USA

This photo illustrates different shapes and sizes of feeding needles. Typically, you can use a 2-3" 22 gauge needle for small or hatchling reptiles, a 3-4" 18-20 gauge for medium sizes, and a 5-6" 18 gauge for larger reptiles. Photo by the author.

A photo illustrating relevant anatomy of the mouth and throat. Note the open glottis (airway). Beyond this is all esophagus. The position of the glottis in relation to the esophagus is similar in snakes, lizards, and turtles. Photo by the author.

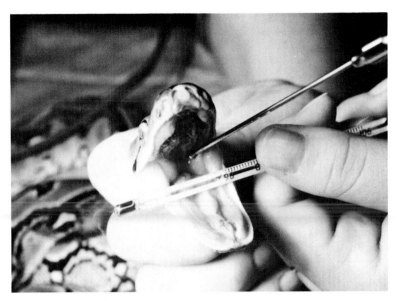

The ball tip of the feeding needle is gently manipulated into the mouth. A gag can be used to open the mouth. With minimal practice the ball tip can be manipulated into the mouth without harming oral tissue or teeth. The tip is passed over the glottis against the roof of the mouth and downward toward the esophagus. Photo by the author.

A lizard can often be incited to open its mouth by gently tapping the end of its snout. Lizards with dewlaps, such as green iguanas, can sometimes be encouraged to open their mouths by simply pulling down on the dewlap. Once open, the stem of a long cotton swab can be used to prevent the lizard from closing its mouth. Photo by the author.

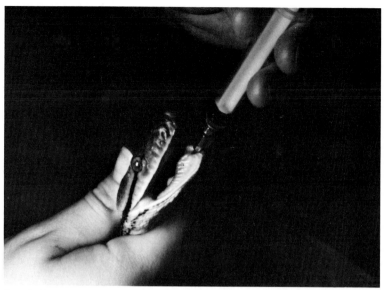

Once inside the mouth, the needle is directed over the glottis and slid against the back of the throat down the esophagus. Photo by the author.

With the reptile in an upright position, the liquid is injected slowly into the back of the throat . After injecting, gently slide back out being careful not to pull if caught on teeth (this rarely happens). Once the needle has been withdrawn, let the reptile go to swallow on its own. Flush the needle with warm water to prevent clogging. The needle can be sterilized by boiling in water for 5 - 8 minutes. Photo by the author.

31

As with snakes, a feeding needle will allow for easy oral administration of medication in lizards. Photo by the author.

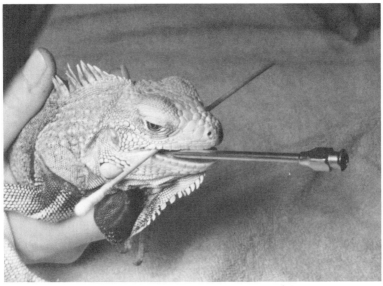

Once inside the mouth the feeding needle is inserted slowly to the back of the throat. Photo by the author.

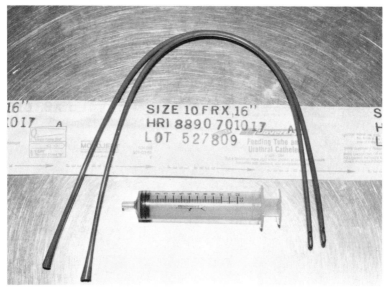

1) Red rubber tube. Photo by the author.

2) The mouth is gaped open by using a steel rod, glass thermometer, metal probe, ball point pen, etc. This is done gently so as prevent injury to the teeth. Certain snakes which tend to be aggressive may also readily open their mouth on their own. Photo by the author.

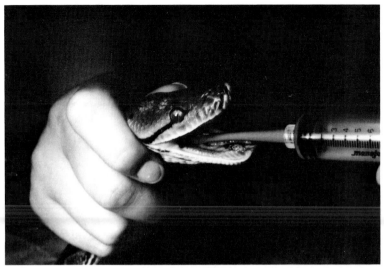

3) The catheter, lubricated with water, is introduced over the glottis, guided against the roof of the mouth, and passed back into the esophagus gently for several inches or until it is 1/3 the distance from snout to vent. Medication is injected while the reptile is held upright. If excessive resistance is encountered, without forcing, re-position the catheter. To administer larger volumes to lizards, pass the tube slightly less than the distance from the tip of the nose to the last rib or just under 1/2 snout to vent length. Photo by the author.

4) The catheter is withdrawn, avoiding any snagging of teeth. The catheter is then flushed with warm water to prevent clogging. Sterilize by storing in alcohol but rinse thoroughly by flushing with water before using again. Photo by the author.

ADMINISTRATION OF DRUGS USING A TIPPED SYRINGE

Unlike snakes, most lizards and turtles use their tongues to manipulate food and facilitate swallowing. This feature allows for medications, especially liquids, to be given orally. A gag can be used to open the mouth, or the edge of the syringe tip can be used to gently tease the mouth open. Once open, the syringe tip is slid to the corner of the mouth to place the medication as far back behind the glottis as possible. Medications are given <u>slowly</u> to allow the tongue to move the drug into position to be swallowed.

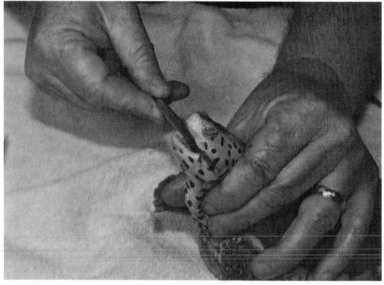

1) A turtle's mouth is gently forced open using a small stainless steel probe as a gag. This photo also illustrates the best way to hold the head of a turtle while medicating. The forefinger and thumb are slid behind the jaw to allow a firm hold while the turtle is unable to withdraw its head. Pressure is applied to the corners of the jaw or just behind the jaw and not to the throat. Photo by the author.

2) The edge of the tip of this 1cc syringe is used to gently pry the jaws open and is then introduced into the turtle's mouth. Photo by the author.

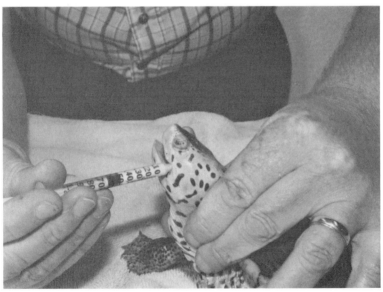

3) Once opened, the syringe tip is slid to the corner of the mouth. The drug is administered slowly to prevent choking. Photo by the author.

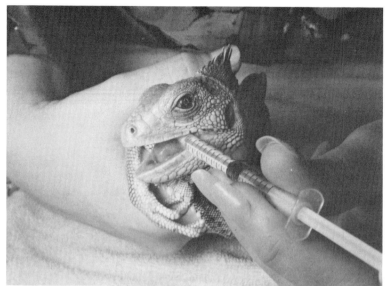

4) The tip of the syringe is used to gently tease open the mouth of the iguana. The tip is then positioned in the corner of the mouth before medication is administered. Photo by the author.

5) The administration of drugs in the food of turtles and tortoises is quite acceptable, especially in shy animals. Always try to hide the medication in a quantity of food that is likely to be completely ingested. Photo by Philippe de Vosjoli.

Other Practical Tips for the Administration of Drugs and Medication

DOSING SMALL REPTILES

Whenever possible, an accurate and precise dose should be arrived at based upon the weight of the reptile. In some cases, especially with very small reptiles, this is difficult to do. The following methods have been employed in such cases:

A) **"Dusting" food items** - Flagyl® tablets may be crushed and food items like pinkies for hatchlings or crickets for lizards can be lightly rolled in the powder. An alternative method is to place the food item in a small bag with the powder and shake. Since overdosage is a potential problem, don't force any more powder to stick to the food item than would naturally do so. The obvious disadvantage to this method is measuring a precise dose, but many individuals have employed this method without apparent harm. Flagyl® is quite bitter and may not be eaten by some reptiles.

B) **Liquids to large groups** - With liquid products such as Panacur®, it is easy to measure and administer a precise dose to a small reptile with a feeding needle. Let's say you are faced with wanting to give Panacur® to a group of 200 anoles. Hiding the product in the drinking water isn't effective because there is a differential rate of consumption by each individual and the drug tends to settle out of the water. To dose such a small animal, a representative weight (i.e., 8 grams) is taken. Panacur® is dosed at 25 mg/kg or 10 mg/lb. There are 454 grams per pound, so this 8 gram reptile weighs 0.017 lbs and the dosage would be (0.017 lbs x 10 mg/lb) 0.17 mg per reptile. Panacur® suspension contains 100 mg/ml so you could add 0.1 ml Panacur® (10 mg) to 2.5 mls of water and now you have a mixture of which 1 ml = 4 mg Panacur®. Since 1 ml contains approximately 20 drops, then one drop will contain 0.2 mg Panacur® which is near our target dose of 0.17 mg. This suspension can then be given with an eye dropper to the entire herd in assembly line fashion, giving each lizard approximately one drop orally. This method works very nicely with drugs that have a wide range of safety. If a narrow range of safety is a characteristic of the drug you wish to administer, then this would not be a good method.

"SHOTGUN" THERAPY FOR WILD-CAUGHT SPECIMENS

The author bases all his treatments on a diagnosis followed by an appropriate treatment. However, in the case of reptiles that are almost always heavily parasitized, dosing with Panacur® and Flagyl® in otherwise healthy specimens will relieve the bulk of the parasite load. Most parasitic problems in recent imports are created by nematode and protozoan parasites. By reducing this stress, many importers feel that the imports are able to adjust and acclimate more easily.

Reptiles that tend to be heavily parasitized are:
1) Imported pythons, particularly ball and Indonesian pythons
2) Water snakes and garter snakes
3) Indigo snakes
4) Most imported Asian snakes, including ratsnakes, sunbeam snakes, and vine snakes
5) Monitor lizards
6) Anoles
7) Imported medium-to-large iguanas
8) Most tropical forest lizards
9) Fence lizards
10) True chameleons
11) All wild-collected turtles

In the author's experience, this list reflects reptiles that have consistently had parasite problems. However, other reptiles may also be heavily infested, particularly species from humid tropical areas.

HOW TO ADMINISTER DRUGS RECOMMENDED FOR PARASITICIDAL USE IN REPTILES

Whenever possible, the best route is to administer a drug directly to the animal, not to hide it in food. The chart below indicates that most of the recommended drugs can be hidden in food, but due to variable rates of uptake by the body, it is better to administer it directly.

When administering small volumes, such as with oral Panacur®, Flagyl®, and ivermectin, the author prefers to use the ball-tipped, stainless steel feeding tubes (see illustration). The ball tip can be gently manipulated into the mouth and the tip guided as deep as it will go in the back of the throat. Larger volumes (over 1cc) can be given with a # 12 French red rubber feeding tube. The author prefers using a method that requires gagging the mouth and guiding the lightly lubricated tube to a depth of at least 8-10 inches in larger reptiles (see illustration).

Injections should be given deep, subcutaneously or intramuscularly, by an experienced person, on the lateral side of the body, one third of the way down the body from the head. Because injections can cause tissue irritation and discomfort, the author uses this route only in extremely fractious animals where it might be dangerous to administer it orally. To repeat, it is always preferable to administer these drugs orally.

METHODS OF ADMINISTRATION

Drug	Drug Form	Ball-Tipped	Stomach Tube	Injectible	Hide in Food
Panacur®	Suspension 100 mg/ml	++	Okay, but not usually needed	N/A	+
Droncit®	Tablets & injectable	Tablets can be crushed and mixed in water	Same as ball-tipped tube	+	+
Flagyl®	Liquid, tabs, injectable	++	++	+	+
Ivermectin	Oral suspension or injectable	++	Not required, give with feeding needle	+	+
Albon®	Oral 5% suspension or injectable	++	++	+	Not recommended; can accumulate as it is dosed daily

++ *PREFERRED*
+ *ACCEPTABLE*

40

Ancillary Treatment of Parasites: Quarantine, Dietary, and Environmental Aspects

The treatment of parasites should actually be termed the "control" of parasites, as this is a multi-factorial process including:
1) quarantine of affected or new reptiles,
2) treatment of environmental factors where applicable,
3) control of food as a source of parasites, and
4) treatment of affected reptiles.

QUARANTINE PROCEDURES

All new reptiles should be contained in an area separate, or even better, removed from the main facility. A typical quarantine period should be at least 30 days. Research done by Lloyd (1992) indicates that other health concerns, such as paramyxovirus, may take up to 90 days to manifest. The longer the quarantine the better. During this time, the reptiles should be checked for parasites by:
1) direct examination for mites/ticks,
2) visual examination of stools,
3) fecal examinations, and
4) sputum examination, if respiratory distress is observed.

Affected animals are best removed to a treatment room for the appropriate therapy before eventually being introduced into the main colony, which has already been deemed parasite-free.

ENVIRONMENTAL

As specific treatments are discussed throughout the text, environmental factors will be pointed out and discussed. A simple example of their importance is observed with parasites such as mites that reproduce and increase in the environment surrounding the reptile. To help eliminate parasites with direct life cycles, appropriate maintenance of reptile enclosures and setups will be required.

CONTROLLING FOOD AS A SOURCE OF INFESTATION

As was discussed earlier in great detail, many animals are intermediate hosts for some parasites and, as such, can pass these parasites on to a non-infected host who dines on such prey. One example would be a garter snake eating an earthworm that could be an intermediate host for capillaria, roundworms, etc.

Freezing pre-killed prey

Most parasites are destroyed by freezing for a period of time. Remember that many life stages of the parasite passed into the environment, such as eggs, oocysts, and larvae, are somewhat fragile and cannot survive for long periods. Fish, frogs, mice, rats, birds, lizards, etc., can all be frozen prior to feeding. How long do they need to be frozen? Good question, as little research has been done on this. Frye (1991) recommends that snakes fed to other snakes, thus representing a potential direct source of parasites, should be frozen for 30 days. Freezing food three to four days is enough to eliminate flukes, but not protozoa. As a rule of thumb, freezing for at least 30 days should eliminate most parasites.

Scenting alternate prey

Another method to reduce parasite exposure by feeding is to scent food less likely to harbor parasites with the scent of preferred prey (which may be infested with parasites). Many people train their lizard-eating snakes to eat mice instead of lizards (which are often highly parasitized), by initially applying the scent of lizard skin to pre-killed and washed mice. A hognose snake that eats mice may be better off than eating wild-caught frogs or toads (Frye, 1973).

Treating rodent colonies

Colonies of mice can be made parasite free by: 1) doing composite fecal exams on the colony, and 2) administering drugs such as ivermectin to the mouse/rat colonies to eliminate nematode parasites. One method of dosing ivermectin in mice and rat colonies is to combine one part of the 1% Ivomec® (MSD AGVET 10 mg/cc) with 5 parts of water and spray the rodents lightly. In normal grooming the rodents will ingest adequate levels of the ivermectin to eliminated nematode parasites. It would be advisable to treat the colony twice at 10-14 day intervals. To prevent ingestion of the ivermectin by the reptiles, the treated rodents should not be fed for at least two weeks after treatment.

Do not re-cycle food items
It is also not a good idea to "re-cycle" food items, i.e., don't take an uneaten mouse from one cage and offer it to another animal. This practice of "muscial food" is one of the main means of spreading many health problems from one animal in a colony to another.

Cryptosporidium signs
Feral mice getting into private rodent colonies has proven to be a source of some common parasitic problems, including *Cryptosporidium*. While it has not been proven that Cryptosporidia in mice can be passed onto reptiles, it has also not been proven otherwise. If a rodent colony is suspected of harboring crytosporidia, then individuals of that colony should be sacrificed and necropsied. If special acid-fast stains and/or histopathology verify the presence of this parasite, it is the author's opinion that the colony should be eliminated.

For successful long term herpetoculture, prey animals such as mice should also have to be checked and treated for parasites. Photo by Philippe de Vosjoli.

Commonly Encountered Reptilian Parasites and Their Specific Treatment

Mites and ticks are the most commonly encountered external parasites, both are irritating as well as possible sources of disease.

MITES (Acariasis)

There are over 250 different species of mites (Mader, 1990) identified which can parasitize reptiles, the most common of which are the snake mite (*Ophionyssus natricis*), the lizard mite (*Hirstiella trombidiiformis*), and the chigger mite.

These mites feed on blood which is required for the transformation from one mite life stage to another. In optimal conditions of high heat and humidity, as is commonly seen in reptile enclosures, they can

Semi-aquatic reptiles such as this *Geomyda spengleri* seldom harbor external parasites. However, with this species as with Asian turtles, treatment with Flagyl•® for protozoans can dramatically improve survival rates of imports. Photo by Philippe de Vosjoli.

reproduce profusely. The mites will tend to accumulate on the reptile's body in areas that afford the most protection, such as under the scales, in the postorbital areas, labial pits, and skin folds near the vent. In a similar manner, they take refuge in every nook, cranny, and crack of the cage and its substrates.

In small numbers, mites may represent a nuisance to the reptile, causing discomfort and agitation. In moderate to severe numbers, mites can cause:

1) anemia
2) rough, eroded, damaged scales which predispose the skin to infection
3) peri-orbital inflammation and swelling
4) depression and anorexia
5) signs related to blood-borne infections
6) difficulties in shedding
7) death

Examples of ticks. Ticks can be disease carriers and it is important to remove these from reptiles. Photo by the author.

TICKS

As with mites, ticks are a nuisance and also a significant source of disease. It is the author's opinion that many tick-laden reptiles develop generalized blood-borne infections. As with mites, the ticks tend to hide under scales, around the eyes, and near the vent.

TREATMENT OF TICKS AND MITES
Manual removal

Once a tick is identified, it can be firmly grasped with forceps or even fingers and pulled out. The key to pulling the ticks out is to not jerk them violently out but to apply firm, steady pulling pressure over the course of several seconds. The tick injects enzymes and other substances onto/into the skin of its host to help liquify the tissue and gain access for feeding. This works to our advantage as this island of tissue will pull away grasped in the tick's mouth. The author has yet to see a pulled tick with its head left attached to its host. One reason why so many people worry needlessly about leaving a head in place is that an inflammatory lump forms after the removal of the

Ticks imbedded in the head of a ball python. Imported specimens of this species are commonly infested with numerous ticks. Photo by the author.

tick. This lump is often misinterpreted as the severed head of a tick. The site of removal can be treated with Betadine® (povidone iodine) or hydrogen peroxide solution. The application of a light layer of a triple antibiotic ointment (i.e., Neosporin®) after cleaning the site is appropriate. The author also routinely treats tick-laden snakes with systematic antibiotics due to the high incidence of infection associated with ticks.

Mites can be removed by gently bathing or rinsing the animal off with tepid water. Extended soaking is a common method employed by many reptiles to drown their mites. While somewhat effective, the reptile may develop skin lesions from excessive soaking and will be exposed to new mites when leaving the soaking container.

The presence of mites and, to a lesser extent, ticks requires a thorough cleaning of the cage and its substrates. Cleaning the cage with a solution of soapy water and household bleach (1 tsp per gallon) is an excellent disinfectant for parasites of all types. Replacing chips, rocks, corncob, etc., with newspaper during treatment is also indicated. Newspaper can be easily and frequently changed while offering few hiding areas for ticks and mites. Branches, shelters, rocks, and other porous objects need to be disinfected by soaking in a 5% bleach solution or eliminated.

The following drugs/insecticides have all been recommended for treating mites and ticks after manual removal.

Ivermectin
Ivomec®, at a dose of .02 cc/kg per os, or essentially 1 drop orally per pound, once every two weeks, has been touted to eliminate ticks and mites that feed on the treated host. The hypothesis of action is that the ivermectin will circulate in the blood stream, and the feeding tick/mite will ingest it when feeding. To date, the author has found that ivermectin has little to no effect on ticks/mites when used in this manner. It is thought that the levels of ivermectin in the reptile's blood stream are not consistently maintained over a long enough period so that all feeding forms of the ticks/mites are exposed. As

mentioned earlier, Rosskopf (1992) has reported good results in snakes when a dosage of 0.2 mg/kg is administered by subcutaneous injection once a week for three weeks. Abrahams (1992) reported excellent results in snakes when a dilute ivermectin spray was used on the snakes and their caging. He prepared the spray by adding 1/2 cc (5 mg) of injectable ivermectin (Ivomec®, 10 mg/cc, MSD AGVET) in one quart of water. Abrahams reported not having to repeat treatment for the mites after one spray.

No-Pest® strips/Vapona® impregnated strips

The dichlorvos pest strips are still a safe and effective method for the treatment of mites, especially with individual reptiles. The procedure involves cutting a small piece of the strip (without directly handling it), perhaps one-eighth of the strip and placing it in a jar or similar container so that the reptile does not come into direct contact with it. Several holes are punched in the lid to allow vapors to escape. Mites are extremely susceptible to this insecticide and exposure of three hours at a time two or three times weekly for two or three weeks is usually adequate. The author removes the water dish while treating, but the reptile and all cage implements remain in the enclosure.

The author has used these strips for over 15 years without any known adverse effects. However, their use has fallen out of favor over the last few years for several reasons. The most common reason is that people report that they did not work, that is, they did not eliminate the mites completely. The reason for most failures that the author has investigated is that the user was using an inadequate number of containers and also doing a poor job of cleaning. Regardless of method, routine cleaning, even changing paper every other day, is a must. You cannot hang an entire No-Pest® strip in a room with several cages and expect to get adequate penetration of the vapors into each and every cage. Every cage must have a No-Pest® container in it twice a week for two or three hours. When 1/8th of a strip was mentioned, this is adequate for a 20 gallon cage, but a very large cage will require a larger piece of No-Pest® strip. Frye (1991) recommends using a 6 mm piece of strip (about 1/5th of an inch) per 10 cubic feet.

No-Pest® strips are not without potential side-effects as these are organophosphate insecticides. The only clinical cases seen by the author were lizards that had been exposed to entire strips for more than 24 hrs. Symptoms included twitching of the extremities and difficulty in coordinating movement. These signs were alleviated by an appropriate dose of atropine. No-Pest® strips have less effect on ticks than mites. They will kill ticks, but manual inspection and removal is essential.

Trichlorfon Spray

Dilutions of this cattle insecticide (Trichlorfon, ChemTronics Inc., Leavenworth, KS or Neguvon, Cutter Animal Health, Mobay Corp., Shawnee, KS) have been proven in limited studies to be an effective agent for treating mites. The most impressive study to date was headed by Donal Boyer, supervisor of reptiles at the Dallas Zoo. In this study, over 600 snakes were treated, with only one death.

The most satisfactory protocol was to prepare a 0.16% solution which can be prepared by adding 8 mls of the stndard 8% stock solution to 400 mls of water in a spray bottle. After cleaning the cage, it is set up with newspaper and sprayed with the trichlorfon and allowed to dry and air out before placing the snake back inside. The researchers warned against using a cage that is airtight or that cannot adequately dry out. The snake is then lightly, but thoroughly, sprayed, including the eyes and labial pits, attempting to get as little as possible into the mouth. Water is withheld for 24 hours, so that a soaking snake won't ingest trichlorfon that dissolves in the water. A second treatment is recommended in ten to fourteen days. The diluted spray seems to remain effective for 30 days.

The author has used this product on approximately 50 reptiles, including snakes and iguanas with excellent results. No untoward effects have been noted. The study indicated that geckos are sensitive to this drug, and it should not be used on these lizards.

CONCLUSIONS FOR THE CONTROL OF MITES AND TICKS

For an individual reptile or very small group of reptiles, the No-Pest® strips are effective and easy to use. As stated previously, the author has had excellent results using these strips with no untoward effects. Large reptile collections present a problem when trying to prepare, rotate, and use these strips.

For large reptile collections the author would recommend the use of the trichlorfon spray at the dosage and methods of application listed previously. When used correctly, trichlorfon has been proven to be relatively safe. The potential for toxicity is present if used incorrectly or in a weakened host.

Ivermectin in a spray form is a very interesting idea, and may prove to be the best method. This method bypasses the problems encountered injecting ivermectin for mite control, as it ensures uniform exposure to the drug.

It cannot be reiterated enough; none of the described methods of control of ticks/mites will be effective if thorough cleanings and frequent substrate changes are not provided.

Northern blue-tongue skinks (*Tiliqua scincoides intermedia*). The giant skinks including the Australian blue-tongues and the Solomon Islands prehensile-tailed skink (*Corucia zebrata*) are very susceptible to infestation by snake mites. Photo by Philippe de Vosjoli.

Internal Parasites

NEMATODES

There are over 500 identified reptilian nematodes, with most occurring in the stomach, small intestine, and large intestine. Certain larval forms are also found in the esophagus, lungs, and other unusual locations due to their migration as larvae. Pathological and deleterious effects are not always seen. Lesions are produced either as larvae migrate through organ systems or by adults entrenched in the gastrointestinal tract. Congregations in large numbers can result in organ obstruction, loss of nutrients, tissue destruction, and the introduction of bacteria.

A) **Roundworms** (*Ophiascaris* and *Polydelphis* sp. in snakes, and *Sulcascaris* & *Anqusticaecum* in chelonians)

Ascarids (roundworms) are very common reptile parasites. They have an indirect life cycle and require intermediate hosts. Roundworms are acquired by ingesting intermediate hosts such as frogs, fish, amphibians, lizards, rodents, and marsupials.

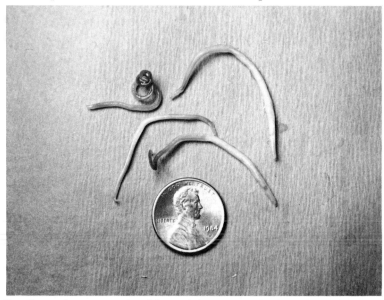

Roundworm larvae regurgitated by an Arizona mountain kingsnake (*Lampropeltis pyromelana*). They have an indirect life cycle and require an intermediate host for successful reproduction. Photo by the author.

51

Reptiles can tolerate moderate loads as these parasites remain passive (not attached) in the GI tract, etc. The most common effect is a secondary malnutrition as these parasites can absorb and steal up to 40% of the usable nutrients available to the host. In a stressed animal that is not eating well, this loss of nutrients can be significant. Impactions of the GI tract, bile ducts, and pancreatic ducts can occur with large parasitic loads. Roundworm larvae migrate through various organ systems as part of their life cycle which can lead to purulent, ulcerative, and inflammatory lesions in the lung, trachea, and other sites. This creates an opportunity for secondary bacterial infections.

Diagnosis is usually based on finding thick-walled eggs in fecal flotations, but in heavy infestations adult worms may be passed in feces or regurgitated contents. Roundworms and tapeworms are the only common endoparasites that can be seen by the naked eye as adults. They appear as round, white, spaghetti-like worms ranging from 1/2 inch to 4 - 6 inches.

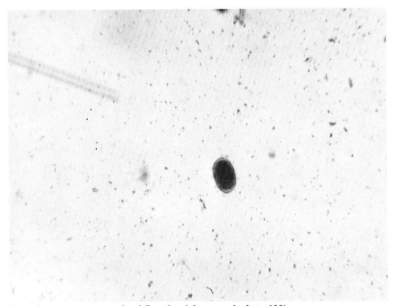

Roundworm egg seen on fecal flotation (photographed at x100).

Treatment consists of giving Panacur® (fenbendazole) at a dosage of 25 mg/kg orally, once every two weeks for two to three treatments. Because this parasite has an indirect life cycle, the reptile cannot re-infest itself. If food sources are the intermediate hosts then options such as 1) considering other food sources, 2) freezing food items first, or 3) de-parasitizing food colonies should be considered.

B) **Hookworms** (*Kalicephalus* sp., snakes; *Oswalsocruzia* sp., lizards; *Camallanus* sp.; and *Spineoxys contortus* sp., fresh water turtles)

Hookworms are parasites with a direct life cycle and are very common in reptiles. These parasites have very little host specificity and can pass to a number of potential hosts. The larvae that hatch from the eggs passed from the host can penetrate skin or gain entrance via contaminated food or water. In captivity tremendous loads can build up in relatively short time periods.

Hookworms can be found anywhere from the esophagus to the rectum. These parasites attach themselves to the intestinal lining and

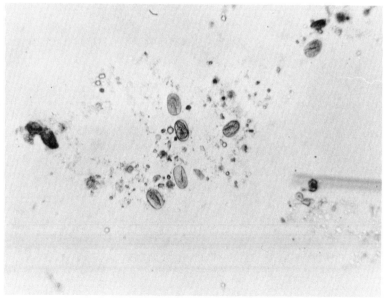

Hookworm eggs seen on fecal flotation (photographed at x100). Photo by the author.

feed on blood. This can lead to 1) hemorrhagic ulcers, 2) severe inflammation, 3) anemia, 4) peritonitis, and 5) an opportunity for bacteria to invade.

Diagnosis is based on finding thin-walled oval eggs on fecal flotation. Bloody and/or mucus-laden stools are a common finding. These worms are not visible to the naked eye.

Treatment consists of giving Panacur® (fenbendazole), at a dosage of 25 mg/kg, once weekly for at least two to three treatments. Strict cleanliness, prompt removal of feces, and frequent changing of bedding materials are steps required to prevent larvae hatching from eggs from gaining direct access to the host. Repeat fecals should be checked at least twice.

C) **Pinworms** (*Oxyurus* sp.)
Pinworms are very common, especially in lizards and turtles. These parasites have a direct life cycle and are acquired by exposure to fecally contaminated food and water.

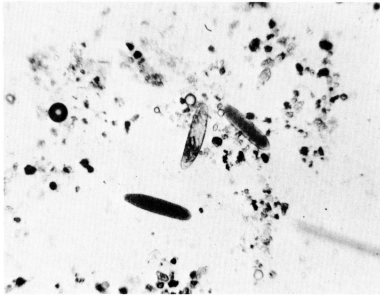

Pinworm eggs (ova) as seen on fecal flotation (photographed at x100). Photo by the author.

Pinworms usually live in the lower GI tract and cause little overt disease. Obstruction and impactions have been reported in iguanas and tortoises.

Diagnosis is based on finding eggs on fecal flotation. Treatment consists of giving Panacur® (fenbendazole) orally, at a dose of 25 mg/kg, once every two to three weeks until negative stools are obtained.

Mouse pinworms are often seen in stools of rodent-eating reptiles. These eggs came from the ingested rodent and the eggs are passed through the GI tract. Mouse pinworms do not cause disease in reptiles.

D) **Stomach worms** (*Physaloptera* sp.)
This parasite occurs almost exclusively in lizards that eat the intermediate hosts (ants). The indirect life cycle with ants as the inter-

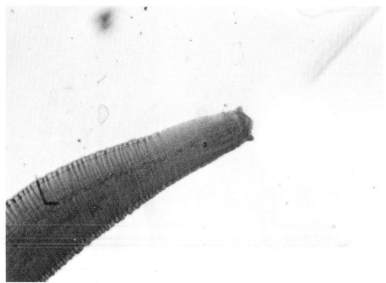

Larva of stomach worm (*Physaloptera*) viewed under the microscope (photographed at x100). This parasite occurs almost exclusively in ant-eating lizards. Photo by the author.

mediate host limits this parasite to lizards who dine on ants as their staple diet, like horned lizards *(Phrynosoma)*.

Stomach worms can cause inflammation and obstruction of the GI tract.

Diagnosis is based on finding eggs on fecal flotation. Treatment consists of giving Panacur® (fenbendazole), at 25 mg/kg, given once every two weeks until negative fecals are obtained.

E) **Lungworms** *(Rhabdias* sp. in snakes, *Entomelas* sp. in lizards) The snake lungworm has a direct life cycle and is a common parasite found in frogs, toads, snakes and chameleons. The larvae that hatch from eggs can gain entrance to the host by percutaneous penetration and by ingestion of fecally contaminated food and water, similar to hookworms.

Lungworms generally have limited effects on the host. Like hookworms, their direct life cycle allows them to build up in large numbers. A "verminous" pneumonia, characterized by gaping mouth, wheezing, and exudate from the trachea, can be seen in heavily infested or extremely stressed animals. The author has confirmed reports from breeders that they had poorly nourished or "double-clutched" snakes dying from such a verminous pneumonia.

The lizard lungworm, *Entomelas*, has a very similar life cycle and behavior, and causes symptoms similar to those of the snake lungworm, *Rhabdias*. Diagnosis is made by finding characteristic eggs in fecal floats, or larvae and ova in sputum. If a snake that has been gaping its mouth is found dead with excessive sputum containing larvae, it is due to these *Rhabdias* lungworms.

The recommended treatment is Panacur® (fenbendazole) at 40-50 mg/kg (a slightly higher dose than with the other nematodes) or with ivermectin at 0.2 mg/kg orally. Either product needs to be given once every two weeks for at least two to three treatments. As with other direct life cycle parasites, strict cleaning, removal of fecal matter, and good hygiene are required.

F) **Strongyloides**

This parasite is similar to *Rhabdias,* but exerts its effects primarily in the GI tract. *Strongyloides* has a direct life cycle, and larvae hatching from eggs gain access to the body by percutaneous penetration and oral ingestion of fecally contaminated food and water.

Diarrhea due to GI irritation is the most common symptom, often with mucus-laden stools. The infective larvae migrate through the lungs of the host and, occasionally, respiratory distress is noted.

Diagnosis is based on finding larvae, not eggs, in fresh fecal samples. Many fecal samples might contain larvae from eggs that were passed and hatched. However, a fresh sample (collected within minutes of passage) that contains larvae instead of eggs is usually *Strongyloides.* Eggs, when seen, are thin-walled and contain larvae and are very similar to those of *Rhabdias* and *Entomelas.*

Treatment consists of giving Panacur® (fenbendazole) orally, at 25 mg/kg, once every two weeks, for at least two or three doses. Due to the direct life cycle, strict cleaning and hygiene is required.

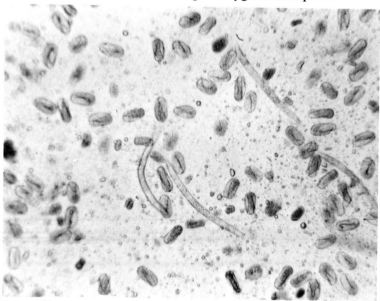

Strongyloides **larvae among eggs characteristic of** *Strongyloides* **or** *Rhabdias.* **Larvae found in fresh stools are more characteristic of** *Strongyloides.* **Photo by the author.**

G) **Hepatic worms** (*Capillaria* sp.)
Capillaria are seen in lizards and snakes. These parasites have an indirect life cycle (perhaps direct as well) and are acquired by ingestion of the intermediate host. The author has primarily found these in garter and water snakes that have eaten earthworms.

Heavy parasite loads can cause reduced hepatic function in affected reptiles.

Diagnosis is made by finding operculated (football shaped with knobs on both ends) eggs on fecal floats.

Treatment consists of giving Panacur® (fenbendazole) orally, at 25 mg/kg, once every two weeks for at least two or three treatments.

H) **Filarial nematodes** (*Oswaldofilaria, Foleyella, Macdonaldius*)
Filarial nematodes are either rare or rarely diagnosed in reptiles. They have an indirect life cycle and are transmitted by arthropods such as ticks or mosquitos and live in the blood stream of the host.

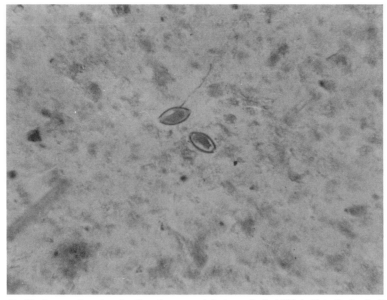

Capillaria **eggs viewed under the microscope (photographed at 100x). Note the football shape and operculated ends. Photo by the author.**

Effects on the host are variable as they are normally found in the blood stream of certain hosts, particularly boids, colubrids, vipers of western Mexico, and in old world chameleons. Problems relating to the circulatory system as with heartworm disease in dogs is possible. In aberrant hosts these filarial worms can migrate and cause blisters and ulcers of the skin.

Diagnosis is based on finding the filarial worms on direct examination of blood smears.

Treatment is accomplished by giving ivermectin at 0.2 mg/kg orally, once every two weeks for two to three treatments.

PROTOZOANS

The protozoan parasites are very common in reptiles. There is some controversy as to the significance of some of these protozoans, as they are so common as to suggest that they are non-pathogenic. The protozoans we will be discussing all have direct life cycles and thus can build up in captivity. As with all parasites with direct life cycles, cleanliness and good hygiene are essential to their control.

A) **Amebiasis**

Far and away the most important protozoan parasite in reptiles is *Entamoeba invadens,* which can be extremely pathogenic. It can exist in carrier animals in which it does no harm, but can be devastating to other reptiles in other geographic regions.

Entamoeba is not rare, but not as common as it has been in years past. It is acquired by ingestion of fecally contaminated food and water and from the environment (cysts are the infective stage). A number of animals that seldom become affected or die can serve as carriers. These include garter snakes, northern black racers, and box turtles. While most turtles are resistant, the giant tortoises are very susceptible. Other resistant groups include eastern kingsnakes, crocodiles, and cobras, possibly as an adaptation that allows them to eat snakes. Most boas, colubrids, elapids, vipers, and crotalids are highly susceptible.

The clinical signs are highly variable, but amoebic dysentery can lead to anorexia, wasting, dehydration, and death. These animals usually are anorectic and often pass mucus-laden, bile-stained, and/or bloody stools.

The diagnosis of *Entamoeba* is made by finding the amoeba, uninucleated trophozoites, or multi-nucleated cysts in smears of fresh stools.

The drug of choice is Flagyl® (metronidazole), at 25-50 mg/kg, given orally once every two weeks until negative fecal examinations are made. The maximum dose given to tricolor king snakes, indigo snakes, and Uracoan rattlers should be 40 mg/kg.

Some researchers (Frye, 1991) have suggested that this dosage range may be inadequate for the boid snakes. He suggests a dosage of 125 mg/kg. It is very important to change bedding frequently, remove feces promptly, and observe proper hygiene.

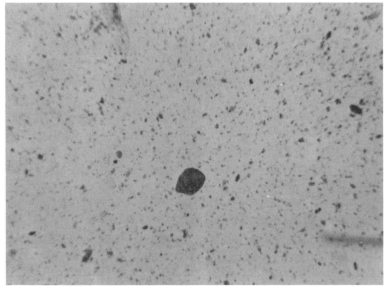

Trophozoites and cysts of *Entamoeba* on a direct smear viewed under the microscope (photographed at x100). Photo by the author.

Since carrier animals do exist, the aforementioned species that are common carriers should be carefully evaluated before mixing with susceptible species. Many cases of amoebic dysentery were traced back to infected feeder animals or contaminated water.

B) **Coccidia** (*Eimeria, Isospora, Caryospora, Cryptosporidium* sp.) These parasites are common protozoans that are generally acquired by exposure to fecally-contaminated food, water, and the environment.

Coccidia, like most of the protozoans, rarely cause problems in free-ranging animals. Coccidia are another example of a parasite with a direct life cycle that builds up in captivity and is aided by stress, poor hygiene, etc., of its host.

Symptoms vary from animals that are feeding but have mild diarrhea, to reptiles afflicted with severe diarrhea, anorexia, debilitation, and eventual death.

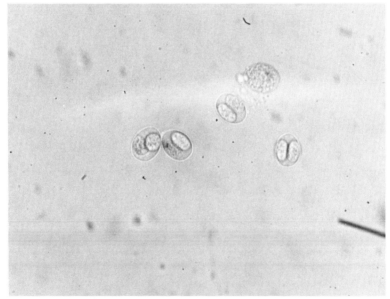

Oocysts of coccidia viewed under the microscope (photographed at x400). These oocysts are small and can be difficult to locate. Photo by the author.

Diagnosis is based on finding oocysts on direct fecal smears or fecal floats of <u>fresh</u> stools.

Treatment consists of orally administering sulfadimethoxine (Albon®) at a dosage of 50 mg/kg daily for three days, stopping three days, then repeating the dosage for three more days. Strict hygiene measures are a must.

C) Cryptosporidiosis

This coccidian parasite strikes fear into the heart of the bravest herper. This is because so little is truly known of the significance of this parasite. Some authorities claim the reptilian parasite to be capable of causing disease in humans. While there is no doubt that cryptosporidia can induce pathology, many authorities feel it is blamed for too much.

Cryptosporidia have been found in lizards and snakes since first reported by Brownstein (1977). Snakes and lizards seem to be the only reptiles in which the parasite will cause disease. Immunocom-

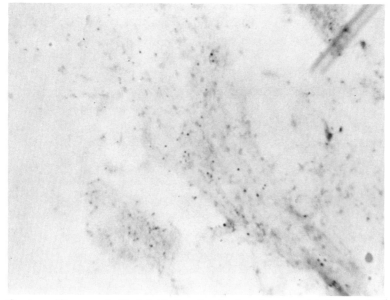

Cryptosporidium oocysts (dark dots) viewed under the microscope (photographed at x100). This parasite is currently not treatable and can be devastating when present in collections. Photo by the author.

promised individuals, such as young and very stressed individuals, are the most commonly affected. In human medicine this disease is most commonly seen in three groups of patients. AIDS patients, due to their poor immune status, are commonly affected. Frye reports that veterinary students and meat packers are commonly affected, but the disease caused is limited to about thirty days, and is characterized by gastrointestinal symptoms. This zoonotic potential impacts the treatment and disposition plan of affected animals as will be discussed.

If healthy specimens are exposed to cryptosporidia, they may become affected by a mild diarrhea for 2-4 weeks or may be completely asymptomatic. Affected animals can become carriers that shed the protozoal agent for up to a year or longer. For obvious reasons, affected animals need to be strictly isolated from the rest of a reptile collection.

As with the other protozoans, cryptosporidiosis is contracted by exposure to sporulated oocysts in contaminated food and water, and also the surrounding environment. Its direct life cycle allows for build-up in captivity. Due to this direct life cycle, cryptosporidia pose a direct threat to any or all reptiles that come into contact with them. The life cycle of cryptosporidia is not completely known, but some researchers, the author included, feel that infected mice can transmit the disease to snakes that eat them. If a group of snakes is found to be affected by this disease, then it is recommended that the client have some mice from their colony or supplier sacrificed for examination. Mice can be asymptomatic carriers of cryptosporidia.

The main lesions induced by this parasite cause severe irritation of the stomach wall (snakes) or intestinal wall (lizards) leading to vomiting/regurgitation. Initially, vague signs such as anorexia, listlessness, wasting, and depression may be noted. In snakes, thickening of the stomach wall leads to an inability to retain food, and regurgitation is common. A firm, mid-body swelling is often noted in affected snakes, due to the extreme swelling and thickening of the stomach lining. However, the author has seen several cases where the stomach thickening was noted only on post-mortem exam, and was not observed externally. In lizards, the intestine rather than the stomach is the site of pathology, and the intestinal lining does not become thickened. Death is a very likely consequence in an affected animal, although they may linger on for months or even years.

The author suspects the presence of cryptosporidia in snakes whenever chronic regurgitation is accompanied by:

1) failure to respond to conventional therapy;
2) extreme weight loss (up to 60-70%);
3) depression (may be due to gastrointestinal pain);
4) mucus-laden, cottage-cheesy stools;
5) mid-body firm mass.

The mid-body firm mass, with the aforementioned signs, is almost conclusive evidence of cryptosporidia. Not all snakes, and no lizards, will show this firm mid-body mass. A mid-body firm mass in a snake with no gastrointestinal problems is unlikely to be due to cryptosporidia.

A boa constrictor with an abdominal bulge caused by cryptosporidiosis. Photo by the author.

Diagnosis is difficult, but coccidia-like oocysts can be demonstrated on direct smears. These oocysts are very small and can easily be overlooked. Staining with acid-fast stains or even with the merthiolate mentioned earlier will help to define these tiny oocysts. Stomach flushes or mucous from regurgitated meals can be collected to examine. The author prefers an acid-fast stain (carbol-fuchsin and brilliant green), in which the oocysts will appear as small red organelles on a green background. G. Allen-Tate (1992) recommends staining fresh fecal material as it will have a richer content of oocysts. An impression smear may not be as productive, due to the organism's invasion of the tissue. In difficult cases, where a high index of suspicion exists, but the oocysts cannot be found, then a histopathology slide from a biopsy may be required. Unfortunately, this disease is often diagnosed during a necropsy following the death of the animal. Samples to be submitted for examination should not be frozen, and the fresher the sample, the better. Formaldehyde-preserved tissues will reveal the oocyst, if present.

To date, cryptosporidiosis is thought to have no treatment. Funk (1987) has suggested oral Trimethoprim-Sulfa at 30 mg/kg once daily or 15 mg/kg twice daily orally for seven days. The use of this regimen by the author has not impacted the course of the disease in affected animals. It is not known if the drug or supportive care offered is the most important component of this regimen. Supportive care consists of fluid, electrolyte, and nutrient supplementation. The author has stabilized affected animals by tube feeding a mixture of A/D (Hills foods) and lactated Ringer's solution every 2-3 days. Due to the bleak prognosis and potential for affecting other reptiles it may come into contact with, euthanasia is often suggested as a course of action by veterinarians. Affected individuals retained must be considered to be potentially very contagious and must be strictly isolated. The potential for the handler to be affected should also be considered when making a decision for the disposition of the affected animal.

D) Flagellates
There are numerous species of flagellates and their pathogenicity is questioned. These protozoans (*Hexamita, Trichomonas, Tritrichomonas,* etc.) are commonly found in the gastrointestinal tract of

reptiles. There is controversy over whether these are normal intestinal flora or true pathogens.

The flagellates are acquired by exposure to infective cysts in contaminated food and water, and during copulation. The effects on the body are variable. The author holds the opinion that small numbers of flagellates can be considered to be normal intestinal flora. However, large numbers in the presence of symptoms (diarrhea, mucous or blood in stools, anorexia, etc.) should be addressed.

Diagnosis is made on direct smears. It takes more practice and expertise with a microscope to accurately diagnose these parasites. Lugol's iodine or merthiolate help to highlight these organisms for easier viewing.

Treat with Flagyl® (metronidazole) orally, at 25-50 mg/kg once, with a follow-up dose, if needed, in three to four days.

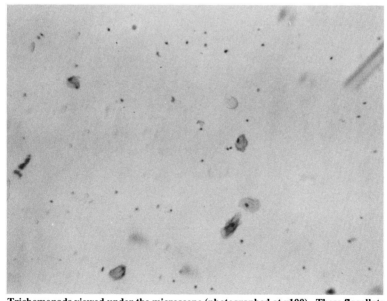

Trichomonads viewed under the microscope (photographed at x100). These flagellate protozoans can be present in many imported reptiles. To better visualize these protozoans, a drop of Lugol's iodine was added to the fecal material before it was mixed with saline on a smear. Photo by the author.

CESTODES

Cestodes, or tapeworms, are common inhabitants of reptiles and amphibians. All reptile cestodes require an intermediate host.

A) Tapeworms

Reptiles acquire tapeworms by ingesting an invertebrate or mammalian intermediate host. As a parasite with an indirect life cycle, there is little risk of these parasites building or spreading within a colony. There usually are few symptoms associated with tapeworms, although in large numbers they can cause: 1) secondary malnutrition by competing for nutrients; 2) inflammation and enteritis due to mechanical irritation; and 3) actual mechanical obstruction.

Diagnosis is made by observing: 1) the eggs on fecal flotation; 2) detection of proglottids in stool; or 3) visibly seeing a tapeworm passed. Like roundworms, tapeworms are large enough to see with the naked eye. Proglottids are small pieces of the adult worm that

Segment of a tapeworm passed by a Nile monitor *(Varanus niloticus)*. Photo by the author.

break off and serve to carry eggs to the outside. They are often described as rice-like and desiccate quickly if another host isn't found.

Treatment is initiated with Droncit® (praziquantel) at 5 mg/kg orally or by injection. A second dose should be given in two weeks.

TREMATODES
This group includes the digenetic and renifer group of flukes. These flukes are commonly observed in the mouth, esophagus, lungs, intestine, and kidneys of their host. Flukes are rarely transmitted in captivity, as they have an indirect life cycle and require an intermediate host.

A) **Flukes**
Flukes are very common especially in indigo snakes, hognose snakes, kingsnakes, water and garter snakes. They are acquired by the ingestion of an affected intermediate host. As snails are a

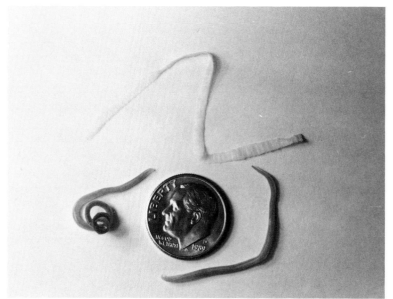

A tapeworm (top) and roundworms. Like roundworms, tapeworms can be seen with the naked eye. Photo by the author.

common intermediate host, flukes are often seen in aquatic turtles and reptiles that eat frogs and fish.

Flukes found orally, within the respiratory system or on superficial tissues, rarely cause any damage. Affected snakes occasionally have a gaped mouth. Renal flukes have been reported in kingsnakes, indigos, tropical rat snakes, bushmasters, and boas, and can cause a chronic interstitial nephritis or other kidney damage.

Diagnosis is by observing adult flukes in the mouth, cloaca, or feces. Ova can be found in the feces, but less commonly. Fluke eggs are large, yellow-brown eggs with a solitary operculum at one end.

Flukes are treated with Droncit® (praziquantel) at 5-8 mg/kg. Adult flukes observed in the mouth, etc., can be gently rolled up with a cotton swab and disposed of. Transmission can be prevented by freezing food items like frogs and amphibians for at least three days prior to feeding.

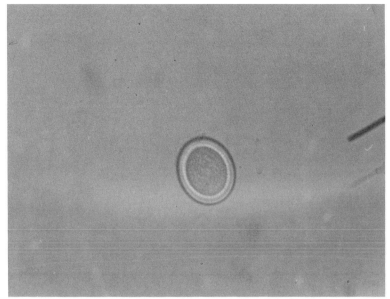

Tapeworm egg as seen on fecal flotation (photographed at x400). Classic tapeworm eggs have several dark "hooklets" in the center of the egg which can be visualized by focusing up and down (see egg reference drawings). Photo by the author.

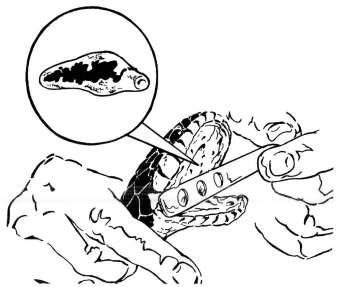

Flukes in the mouth of a snake. Illustration by Glenn Warren.

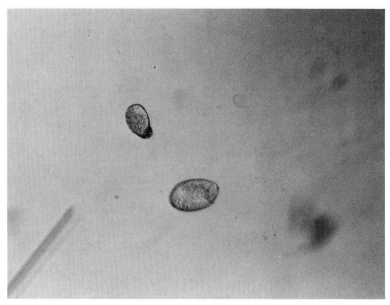

Fluke eggs as seen on fecal flotation (photographed at x100). These are large, heavy eggs, usually operculated at one end. Photo by the author.

PENTASTOMIDS

The pentastomids are a group of parasites that migrate as larvae from the intestinal tract and undergo extensive organ migration. As adults, they tend to be found in the lungs and subcutaneous tissues.

These are not common parasites. *Armillifer armillifer* in pythons and vipers, *Porocephalus* sp. in boids and crotalids, and *Kiricephalus* in colubrids are the most frequently seen species.

These parasites have an indirect life cycle. Eggs containing the larvae are deposited and secreted from the lungs into the sputum and swallowed. The eggs are then passed in the feces, and a suitable intermediate host (insect, rodent, etc.) swallows the egg. The developing larvae become infective nymphs in the intermediate host, and the reptile host feeds on this intermediate host. Extensive larval migration occurs before adults form in the lungs and complete the cycle.

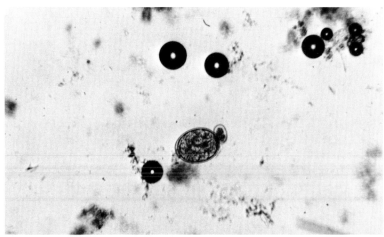

Pentastomid eggs viewed on fecal flotation (photographed at x100). Note the smaller, adjacent hookworm eggs. Photo by the author.

71

Despite large numbers and extensive larval migration, most infestations are without symptoms. In some cases, there can be damage to the tissue during larval migration or when in the lungs.

Diagnosis consists of observation of the adults or by finding eggs on fecal flotation. The adults are very primitive in appearance, often being described as looking like a prehistoric caterpillar.

Treatment is attempted with ivermectin at 0.2 mg/kg orally for at least two or three doses, two weeks apart.

SUBCUTANEOUS PARASITES

The most common types of parasites found in a lump just under the skin are the plerocercoid stage of some tapeworms and, occasionally, a misguided pentastomid.

Regardless of type, a small incision through the skin and into the subcutaneous tissue will result in access to the parasite, which can easily be removed with tweezers. The lesion should be flushed with hydrogen peroxide solution or iodine, and an antibiotic ointment packed in the cavity. If the lesion is extensive, administration of systemic antibiotics should be considered.

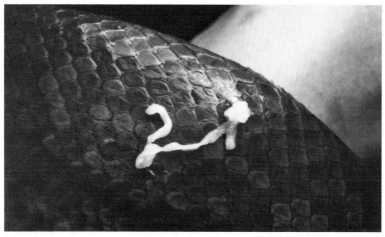

Example of a subcutaneous parasite in the form of a misguided, migrating tapeworm. A small skin incision was made over the site at the fluctuant swelling and the tapeworm was teased out with forceps. Photo by the author.

72

DIAGNOSTICALLY IMPORTANT PARASITES, THEIR INFECTIVE STAGES, AND RELATIVE SIZES

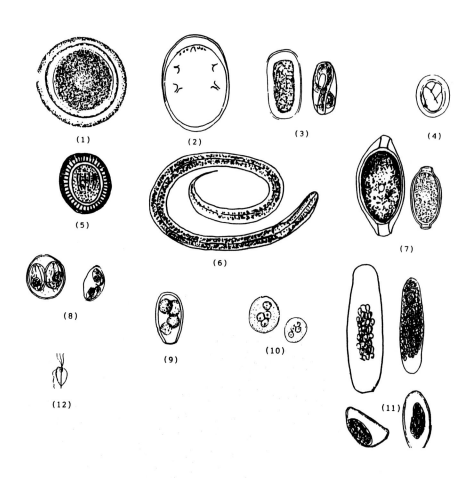

1) Ascarid (roundworm) ova
2) Pentastomid ova
3) *Kalicephalus* (hookworm) ova
4) *Rhabdias, Entomela,* or *Strongyloides* ova
5) *Taenia* sp. (tapeworm) ova
6) *Strongyloides* larva

7) *Capillaria* sp. ova
8) *Isospora* cyst (coccidia)
9) *Eimeria* cyst (coccidia)
10) *Entamoeba invadens* cyst (ameoba)
11) Oxyurid sp. (pinworms) ova
12) Trichomonad (protozoan)

Hygiene and the Herpetoculturist

The importance of good hygiene has been mentioned repeatedly in the text. This aspect of reptile care is one of the most neglected and overlooked, yet it is extremely important in maintaining healthy reptiles.

If the health of the reptiles in captive care is not enough motivation, then perhaps the personal health of the herpetoculturist is. Many of the parasites discussed have zoonotic potential (ability to cause disease in humans). Such parasites include cryptosporidia, ascarids, hookworms, pinworms, amoebic organisms, protozoan agents (Giardia, Trichomonas, etc.), certain cestodes, and ticks, to name but a few. This list is not being presented to make the average reptile owner paranoid, but to emphasize the necessity for good hygiene measures.

Good hygiene is just good common sense. The author, in visiting reptile collections around the country, has found the following areas to be the most neglected:

1) **Fecal accumulation** - Simple cage cleaning is all that is required to prevent excessive fecal accumulation. This is more important in cages with poor ventilation. With excessive moisture, feces is also an odor and fungal problem. Breathing ammonia fumes is irritating to all mucous membranes, especially the eyes and lungs.

Substrate choice definitely affects the rate of cleaning. While newspaper is not attractive, it is easy and cheap to remove. Cages that use paper, artificial carpet, etc., are much easier to clean than those employing rocks, gravel, dirt, etc. Rocks and gravel also allow fecal material and urates to filter down into them and get trapped.

2) **Cleanliness** - While it is important to change substrates on a regular basis, the cage must also be cleaned. The author prefers to use a bleach/soapy water mixture. To prepare this mixture the author

mixes 1-2 tsp of dishwashing soap with 1/4-1/2 cup of bleach to one gallon of water. Disinfectants such as Roccal® and Nolvasan® are also good. Cages need to adequately dry to prevent excessive moisture and fungus problems.

3) **Contaminated water** - Water and food dishes, if employed, need to be washed and disinfected on a regular basis. The author suggests changing the drinking water at least twice a week, and washing and disinfecting the dishes at least once every two weeks (more often if soiled). Contaminated water is not only a possible source of parasitic exposure, but is a common source of bacterial problems. The scum in a water dish that has not been treated properly will commonly culture out several bacteria, including the coliforms (*E.coli*) and *Pseudomonas*. The soapy water/bleach mixture will work nicely.

4) "**Musical food**" - A food item refused by one reptile should not be offered to another reptile, especially killed food that has been allowed to sit for several hours.

5) **Lack of effective quarantine** - Many herpetoculturists will place a new reptile in a separate container for a few days and, if eating well with no regurgitation, etc., will introduce it into their main colony. It used to be agreed that a 30 day quarantine period should be adequate, but research information (Lloyd) has indicated that a 90 day period may be needed to protect against the introduction of viruses, such as paramyxovirus.

6) **Lack of personal hygiene** - Simple hand washing is generally neglected. Washing with household hand soap will generally physically remove all parasites, bacteria, and viruses. For more resistant bacteria and viruses, an average quality anti-bacterial soap will suffice. Sam's wholesale warehouses sell a gallon of anti-bacterial liquid soaps for use on hands for $6.00. In other words, it is not expensive and it is very important that you use it.

APPENDIX I
OTHER SOURCES OF INFORMATION ON REPTILE PARASITES

The following sources are listed for their current publishing dates, excellent photos/illustrations, and relevant information on this topic:

1) Exotic Animal Medicine in Practice, The Compendium Collection, Fifth Anniversary Series, published by Veterinary Learning Systems, 1986.

2) Reptile Care, An Atlas of Diseases and Treatments, by F.L. Frye, D.V.M., M.S. Published by TFH, 1991.

3) The Biomedical and Surgical Aspects of Captive Reptile Medicine, by F.L. Frye, D.V.M., M.S. Second edition in two volumes, published by Krieger publishing, 1991. A more expensive version of 2 with dust cover.

4) Zoo and Wild Animal Medicine, edited by M.E. Fowler, published by B. Saunders Company, 1986, first and second editions.

APPENDIX II
MICROSCOPE SOURCES

The most reasonable and practical source of microscopes I have found is the Edmund Scientific Co., 101 E. Gloucester Pike, Barrington, NJ 08007-1380, 1-609-547-8880. They will send a free complimentary catalog which lists the extensive microscopic equipment they carry. They offer name brands and make their own equipment, ranging from $129.00 to $2,000.00, depending on features. As mentioned in the text, they address what makes one microscope better than another and, best of all, you can buy a basic scope and buy "add-ons" to go with it. For instance, with a basic scope you can add a mechanical microscopic stage for $42.95, or upgrade your lighting source, etc.

A source of used equipment is the equipment departments at nearby hospitals and universities. A large number of such non-profit organizations upgrade their equipment when they have been fully depreciated, and they are no longer a tax deduction. The author has known persons who have obtained very good microscopes from such sources for as little as $50.00.

Another potential source of used equipment is the "for sale" or ad boards at local universities. Many students are required to own a microscope and then sell them after graduating, changing majors, etc. In larger metropolitan areas, there are microscope dealers listed in the yellow pages. Some of these dealers also carry used equipment. These dealers also service and repair microscopes if the need arises.

Regardless of the source, don't buy more than you need, but don't settle for too little if extensive use is planned.

APPENDIX III
UNPUBLISHED RESEARCH
Between 1988 and 1992, the author had the opportunity to treat well over 300 ball pythons. Each of these ball pythons had at least one type of nematode parasite. The first 100 ball pythons were administered a dose of Panacur® (fenbendazole) at the higher end of the dosage scale common in the literature, 50-100 mg/kg. The second 100 were given Panacur® at the author's preferred dose, 10-25 mg/kg. The third 100 were given Ivomec® (ivermectin) at 0.2 mg/kg or 0.02 cc/kg. All products were given orally once every two weeks and follow-up fecals performed. A "cure" was noted when negative fecals were obtained. All snakes were held at 80 - 82 F before and after worming.

The results indicated that: 1) Panacur® at either dosage worked better than Ivomec®; 2) Panacur® worked as well at the lower dosage; and 3) all regimens were safe. It took a minimum of two to three doses of Panacur® (either dosage) and a minimum of three to five doses of ivermectin to produce negative fecals.

The other study performed was on 25 different species of snakes over a similar time span, that all had evidence of protozoal disease in the form of trichomonads. While we have discussed that trichomonads are often a normal colon inhabitant, occasionally they are found in excessive numbers and in the presence of diarrhea, etc. These snakes were administered oral Flagyl® elixir at 25 mg/kg (day one and day ten) and were clear of clinical signs and had dramatically reduced protozoan counts.

While the second study is not well structured because specimen types are different, it does illustrate that the dosage listed at 175-250 mg/kg in the literature is very outdated. Better controls would be necessary to arrive at an exact dosage, which would be useful to avoid excessive doses.

References

Abrahams, R. 1992. Ivermectin as a Spray for Treatment of Snake Mites. Bulletin of the Association of Reptilian and Amphibian Veterinarians. 2(1):1992.

Allen-Tate, G. 1992. Personal communication Colorado State University, College of Veterinary Medicine. Ft. Collins, Colo. 80532.

Barnard, S.M. 1983. A Review of Some Fecal Pseudoparasites of Reptiles. J. Zoo Animal Medicine, 14:79-88.

Boyer, D. 1992. The use of Trichlorfon spray for Mites in Snakes. Bulletin of the Association of Reptilian and Amphibian Veterinarians. 2(1): 2-3, 1992.

Brownstein, D.G., et al. 1977. Cryptosporidium in Snakes with Hypertrophic Gastritis. Vet. Pathol., 14:606-617.

Dinardo, D. 1002. The Effects of Stress on Lizards and Its Application to Captive Management. Fifteenth International Herpetological Symposium. Presented 6/92, in press.

Frye, F.L. 1991. Biomedical and Surgical Aspects of Captive Reptile Husbandry, second edition, in two volumes, Krieger Publishing, Macabar, Fl. 1991.

Funk, R.S. 1987. Implications of Cryptosporidiosis in Emerald Tree boas, Corallus caninus. In M.J. Rosenberg (ed), International Herpetological Symposium, on Captive Propagation and Husbandry, Chicago, Illinois, June 17-20, 1987. pp 139-143.

Funk, R.S. 1988. Herp health hints and husbandry: Parasiticide dosages for captive amphibians and reptiles. Chicago Herp Society newsletter, 23(2):30.

Gillingham, B. 1989. Personal communication. 555 Vista Rio Court, Woodbridge , CA. 95258.

Harvey-Clark, C. 1991. Efficacy of Vercom in the Treatment of Oxyurid Nematodes in Green Iguanas (*Iguana iguana*). Bulletin of the Association of Reptilian and Amphibian Veterinarians. 1(1): 7-8.

Ippen, R. 1972. Problems caused by Parasites in Zoo Specimens. VISZ, 173-186, XIII (translated from German).

Jackson and Cooper. 1981. Diseases of the Reptilia. Academic Press, Inc. Two volumes.

Jacobson, E.R. 1983. Parasitic Diseases of Reptiles. In Kirk, R.W. (ed): Current Vet. Therapy. Vol. 8. W.B. Saunders, Philadelphia.

Jacobson, E.R., Kollias, G.V. 1988. Exotic Animals, Churchill Livinstone, pp. 43-47.

Jacobson, E.R., Kollias, G.V., Peters, L.J. 1983. Dosages for antibiotics and parasiticides in exotic animals. Compendium Cont. Ed. 5:315.

Levine, N. 1982. Textbook of Veterinary Parasitology. 2nd ed. Burgess Publishing Co., Minneapolis, Minn.

Lloyd, M.L. 1992. Ophidian Paramyxovirus - Historical Overview and Current Recommendations on Control. Fifteenth International Herpetological Symposium. Presented 6/92. In press.

Mader, D.R. 1989. Mites and the herpetologist. The Vivarium, 1(4):27-31.

Mader, D.R. 1990. Cryptosporidiosis. The Vivarium, 2(6): 14-15.

Miller, M.J. 1987. Use of Vercom Paste as an Anthelmintic in Reptiles. Bulletin of the Chicago Herp. Society. 22(4): 73-74.

Rossi, J. 1992. Husbandry and Medicine of Small North American Snakes. Proceedings of The North American Veterinary Conference. Vol. 6: 708-709.

Rosskopf, W.J. 1992. Ivermectin as a Treatment for Snake Mites. Bulletin of the Association of Reptilian and Amphibian Veterinarians. 2(1).

Soulsby, E.J.L. 1976. Pathophysiology of Parasitic Infection. Academic Press, New York.

Wakelin, D. 1984. Immunity to Parasites. Edward Arnold publishers.

Williams, J.F., Zajac, A., 1980. Diagnosis of Gastrointestinal Parasitism in Dogs and Cats, published by Purina.

Wright, K. 1992. The Use of Anthelmintics (dewormers) in Captive Herbivorous Reptiles. The Vivarium, 3(6): 23-25.

American Federation of Herpetoculturists

The American Federation of Herpetoculturists (AFH) is a nonprofit organization whose purpose is to represent the interests of herpetoculturists, those individuals involved with the captive husbandry and propagation of amphibians and reptiles.

The AFH was the first organization to publish a full color publication *The Vivarium* magazine, dedicated to the keeping, breeding and enjoyment of amphibians and reptiles. The AFH's primary goal is to provide the information necessary for the continued and responsible relationship between humans, and reptiles and amphibians.

A membership will entitle you to the following:

- A membership with the AFH. An active organization of herpetological hobbyists and professionals.

- A subscription to *The Vivarium* magazine. Six (6) high quality 8 1/2 x 11" issues, published bi-monthly. Each issue contains information on amphibian and reptile field studies, natural history, biogeography, legislative concerns, captive maintenance and breeding, enclosure design, feeding techniques, and veterinary medicine.

- Special Discounts on AFH sponsored programs and merchandise.

Individual Membership in the AFH is $26.00 in the U.S. Foreign Membership is $32.00. For more information write to:

AFH
P.O. Box 1131
Lakeside, CA 92040

* The AFH is not affiliated with Advanced Vivarium Systems